When reading Danny's book, I sensed God saying, "Listen to me, learn from me, live for me, lead others to me." *Spark Teams* emphasizes the evangelization of the sinner, the edification of the saints, the exaltation of the Savior, and the importance of producing a church of faithful believers. As Danny says, instead of working *for* God, we need to be working *with* God. I recommend this book as it will both convict and challenge you.

WENDELL CALDER, founder and director, Local Church Evangelism

Danny Sathyadass has written a thoughtful and inspiring book on Christian ministry and leadership, drawing from his ministry experiences over three decades. He openly shares his lived experiences, calling to ministry, struggles and hardships, errors made, lessons learned, and the process of identifying a ministry that aligns with his spiritual gifts and pastoral heart. The insights shared on discipleship are significant for anyone desiring to grow in Christian discipleship, and the perspectives offered on Christian leadership are applicable to anyone aspiring to Christian leadership. These fresh and thought-provoking ideas, presented with sound biblical principles and theological foundations, are compelling. The book is reflective, clear, and succinct, and ideal for practical, personal application. This must-read book will be a valuable resource to all believers. I pray that many will be blessed and impacted by it.

THOMAS KULANJIYIL, PhD, professor of philosophy, Glen Ellyn, Wheaton, IL

I deeply resonate with Danny's observation that much of our "Christian" endeavors involve perpetually feeding and entertaining crowds and that leaders often derive a false sense of worth and significance as we "bask in the limelight of accolades from the masses." Danny challenges us to disperse the crowds and withdraw to spend time with the Lord, looking to invest ourselves in the disciples around us, "who are likely straining at the oars on a stormy sea."

This book is a practical distillation for active disciple-making teams, written by an Indian with experience in both his homeland and diaspora communities, and with sensitivity to the importance of family.

ROBBY BUTLER, editor of James Nyman's *Stubborn Perseverance* and Steve Smith's *No Place Left* saga

Danny has been planting churches for the last twenty-five years. I was privileged to meet him and be a part of this journey. *Spark Teams* is a collection of more than two decades of experience he has in this arena. His focus on the idea of church as a "team" is incredibly helpful. The wealth of experience and ideas that Danny has learned and explained here through his story make this a useful read for any believer in Jesus.

NEILL MIMS, church planter and coach

Danny Sathyadass has written a helpful book about discipleship principles that will benefit church planters. Written out of the crucible of struggle, failure, and success, he presents a model that encourages the reader to think outside the box. This book is not an ivory tower exposé written for the academy; instead, it is written for the practitioner who needs a new model for discipleship training. Danny, a church planter working primarily in India, presents a model that is not only biblically based but filled with many practical suggestions—a worthwhile read.

DR. DAVID SHERBINO, professor of pastoral ministries, spiritual formation, and thanatology, Tyndale University Graduate School, Toronto, Canada; minister, Presbyterian Church in Canada

Danny Sathyadass, a passionate disciple and insightful leader, has managed to encapsulate all that it means for us to follow the model of Jesus and create an empowering dynamic to form and multiply disciples, leaders, teams, and churches using the frame of teaching, evangelism, adoration, mentoring, and sharing (TEAMS). This book is full of compelling stories, practical wisdom, and actionable steps to help readers implement these ideas. A valuable resource!

RICH ROBINSON, cofounder, Movement Leaders Collective, Creo, and Catalyse Change; author, *All Change*

Recent years have seen a growing interest in the impact of house church movements around the world. *Spark Teams* underlines the value of academic and theological insight when added to years of practical experience. Through Danny's "DIE" acronym—representing drawing, influencing, and empowering—we see the deep commitment to following Christ in his death as our pathway to life. Building from such foundations, with stories from his active involvement in rural and city-based movements, this book demonstrates that simple church movements are timely and solidly biblical. *Spark Teams* is of great value to anyone drawn to this pathway of growth through discipleship.

DRS. TONY AND FELICITY DALE, authors, *The Rabbit and the Elephant*

Systematic theologians excel in studying the entirety of God's Word on select subjects. However, seminary colleagues often notice a weakness in local church practice. Why? Because each context brings unique questions for applying biblical principles in spiritual and corporate life. Danny Sathyadass hovers between the universal and the local, the prescriptive and the descriptive, the normative and the contextual, to find principles for healthier local church existence, growth, and function. Indeed, there is one message and mission, but many ministries and methods. Through reading this book, any Christian with a heart and mind to know and learn will find that their hands and feet soon explore the relevance of the early church to their contemporary situation.

RAMESH RICHARD, PhD, ThD, founder and president, RREACH; professor, Dallas Seminary; founder, TOPIC; convener, GProCommission

In this book, Danny Sathyadass is speaking my language. Through stories of his own experience, the experiences of others (past and present), and by leading us into Scripture, Danny reminds us of our identity and purpose as the body of Christ: disciples who make disciple-makers. He does this not by detailing cultural practices of "church" or proven strategies for "success" but by following the example of Jesus and his "team" of twelve. Tying his theology and practice to that of Wesley, he lays out mission-critical practices in disciple-making while encouraging contextualization and being led and empowered by God's Spirit. Sathyadass models a learner's posture, Spirit-led adaptability, and humility as he discloses how God called and gifted him, and shaped a ministry that was very different from what he first imagined. This book is now the latest on my "must-reads" for new—and old—cross-cultural workers.

BECKY STEPHEN, senior director of global engagement, TMS Global

Our world of individualism is as powerful as it is prideful in its influence on society. Demonstrating a "Christian life" through one's words, walk, and worth under the guise of individualism is deceptive. Connectedness between individual believers is at the core of membership in the body of Christ. This body is a dynamic, living organism comprised of believers and not an organization under the leadership of a figurehead. It is a community of *sinners* called to be *saints*, with the *relationship* of sons and daughters and the *responsibility* of servants. The uniqueness of this privilege is best achieved when Christ-followers view each other as vital members of a team under Christ, our federal head.

This substantive, timely, meaningful, and insightful work is the fruit of Danny's labor of love for God, God's Word, and God's people. These characteristics adorn his ardent pursuit of excellence, "sparking teams for change." I am a witness to the outworking of this focused approach in his personal and public life.

To that end, I heartily recommend this model for the growth of God's people and the glory of God in anticipation of Christ's soon return.

DAVID R. ABRAHAM, PhD, adjunct professor, School of Education,

Liberty University

As one who teaches and serves in a disciple-making ministry among young people worldwide, this book is a breath of fresh air. It is loaded with practical biblical insights that help us think outside our culture and traditions. The worldwide (and especially Western) church would do well to consider the power of TEAMS for truly making disciples as Jesus did. Even with the church's desire to be "innovative" and "relevant," more often than not, we end up with a very formatted, traditional, and dare I say, *unbiblical* understanding and practice of what the gathered church was originally meant to be. I have witnessed firsthand Danny's heart, passion, and practice in his own home in India, and I am excited that he is now able to share this with the world.

KRISTOPHER STOUT, executive vice president of international ministries,
Word of Life Fellowship

In this age of the celebrity leader, we need more people who want to serve the needs of a team. I love the leadership dictum which states, "You can go faster by yourself … but you can go further with a team." My friend and colleague Danny Sathyadass has captured this truth in this book. I continually marvel at the truth that Jesus moved *away* from the crowds and *toward* the Twelve. So much so that critics of the early church complained that the disciples had turned the whole world upside down with their teaching. I urge you to carefully read this book with a pencil in one hand and a notepad in the other. Or, better yet, read it together with your whole team!

DR. PAUL PETTIT, director of career services; adjunct professor in
pastoral ministries, media arts and worship, and educational
ministries and leadership, Dallas Theological Seminary

I've known Danny for quite a few years, and I can truly say that his book flows out of who he really is—a genuine disciple of Jesus. *Spark Teams* offers relevant insights, practical applications, and reliable guidance for bridging the discipleship gap in today's church. I wholeheartedly recommend this book to anyone serious about disciple-making.

ALDRIN BOGI, global vice president of programs, Biblica

In this book, Danny, a dear friend and partner, offers a compelling exploration of how the church can spark significant changes in the city. Through this thoughtful and practical guide, he tackles the need for smaller, more intimate church structures. This is not just another book to add to your shelf but a valuable resource for church leaders and planters, especially those seeking to establish house groups.

Drawing from his extensive experience as a pioneer of small-group churches, Danny has spent countless hours grappling with the realities of church growth, membership struggles, and leadership challenges. His insights are rooted in these real-world challenges, making the book relatable and impactful.

Each chapter is simple yet profound, offering practical wisdom that can be applied immediately. Whether you are a pastor, leader, or church planter, you will find this book deeply insightful and an essential tool in your ministry. Danny's message encourages readers to act and test the principles within, to grow the body of Christ, and shape the church into a biblical, New Testament model.

I highly recommend this book for anyone looking to understand how small, Christ-centered teams can revolutionize church life. It is as practical as it is deep, offering both a blueprint and a challenge for the future of the church.

JACOB ISAAC, executive coach and leadership consultant,
TURN Consultants; director, Kerygma

Most Christians, even church leaders, don't do the one thing our Lord mandated: Make disciple-makers! Danny Sathyadass has drawn from Jesus and his disciples' lifestyle to encourage team-building that will move "church" from a maintenance mode to be the unstoppable movement it was meant to be! He reveals the cause and the cost entailed. He contends that church planting is grounded in biblical principles, not merely structural formalities. This calls for sacrificial love and daily obedience that are open to and guided by God's enabling Holy Spirit. Such teams naturally equip, intentionally empower, and spontaneously reproduce. You will observe working models within contextual realities that show gospel relevance and engage graceful strategies. We serve better together, and certainly shine brighter together. May this book inform and ignite us to … spark teams!

CHRIS GNANAKAN, DMin, PhD, DD, director of leadership development, Christar; professor of theology and global studies, Liberty University; South Asia catalyst, church planting, Lausanne Movement

Spark Teams will convince you that small is beautiful and yet complete. This book is biblically based but filled with stories from Danny's own journey over the years, giving it authenticity. In the light of the current hostile climate in India, this structure may be the way forward.

STANLEY MEHTA, chairman and founder, Gateway Ministries International - India

Danny Sathyadass has written an exceptional book on what can happen when Christianity is brought to people free of traditional church structures and methods. Based on the remarkable experience of Radiance Church, the development of an innovative radio ministry, and the proliferation of Radio Home churches in India, it draws out the principles that are applicable to other cultural contexts when discipleship is made both the means and the end of active church life. Practical and down-to-earth, *Spark Teams* is a valuable addition to the literature on how Christians can respond to the post-Christian, globalized, technology-dominated world of today.

GEOFF TRELOAR, PhD, research fellow, Australian University of Theology; author, *The Disruption of Evangelicalism: The Age of Mott, Torrey, McPherson and Hammond*

This is a book about being the church, not in a designated building and with a fixed format, but wherever life happens. It comes out of the author's hard-won personal journey, dwells on central Bible-based truths, and contains many diverse real-life stories. In doing this, it illuminates for us the basic principles of community in, and mission with, Christ. The writing is fresh, crisp, and lively, full of both practical resources and examples. In the spirit of a book built around two simple acrostics, I urge you to

Reserve time to go closely and prayerfully through it;
Enlist others in your sphere of influence to study it;
Arrange times for them to join you and discuss it; and
Discern together what God wants you to do about it.

DR. ROBERT BANKS, author, *Going to Church in the First Century, A Day in the Life of an Early Christian, Paul's Idea of Community,* and *The Church Comes Home*

For our disruptive times, here is a novel, insightful, and challenging book that will compel you to rethink what the church is and the mission of God in the world. A must-read for every church leader, church planter, evangelist, missionary, and lay minister.

SAM GEORGE, PhD, Lausanne Movement; coeditor, *Sharing Jesus with Hindus* and *Asians in Diaspora and Diasporas in Asia*

Spark Teams is a transformative guide that reimagines the church as a dynamic movement of Christ-centered teams. This book is a must-read for anyone passionate about disciple-making and church planting. It offers profound insights into the importance of being led by the Holy Spirit and maintaining a close relationship with God. The real-life stories of disciple-makers and the insider perspective on church planting in the Global South make it an invaluable resource for contemporary church leaders. The strategies and actionable steps provided in the book are both inspiring and practical, encouraging readers to build authentic relationships, create a culture of mutual accountability, and celebrate collective progress. *Spark Teams* is a call to action for all who seek to foster growth and change through reliance on God and collaboration within teams.

DAVID DAYALAN, pioneer and pastor, Gurgaon Christian Fellowship; former vice president of program development, A3 International

SPARK
TEAMS

Disciple-Making
and Being Church
Wherever Life Happens

SPARK
TEAMS

Foreword by
JOSEPH W. HANDLEY, JR.

Afterwords by
VARUGHESE JOHN
& ALAN HIRSCH

DANNY
SATHYADASS

100 MOVEMENTS
PUBLISHING

Library of Congress Control Number: 2025915827

ISBN 978-1-955142-72-4 (print)
ISBN 978-1-955142-73-1 (eBook)

Cover design and interior design by Jude May

100 Movements Publishing
An imprint of Movement Leaders Collective
Cody, Wyoming
www.movementleaderscollective.com

To Mike, Sherrine, and Nikki.
This book is dedicated to you, "so you can know beyond the shadow of a doubt the reliability" (Luke 1:4 MSG) of what I have kept sharing.
Your home was our "house of peace" through this writing journey. Thank you for your love and service.
"God is not unjust; he will not forget your work and the love you have shown him as you have helped his people and continue to help them" (Hebrews 6:10).

CONTENTS

Foreword by Joseph W. Handley, Jr.   xvii

Introduction   xxi

PART ONE - DIE: GOD'S INITIATIVE OF LOVE   1

1   Give Up, Take Up, and Keep Up the Cross of Jesus   3

2.   Draw   17

3.   Influence   27

4.   Empower   41

PART TWO - TEAMS: OUR RESPONSIBILITY AS
                GOD'S CHURCH   55

5.   Rethinking Church   57

6.   Teaching   81

7.   Evangelism   93

8.   Adoration   107

9.   Mentoring   119

10. Sharing   129

Conclusion : Spark TEAMS, Make Disciples, and Be the
             Church Wherever Life Happens   143

Afterword by Varughese John   155

Afterword by Alan Hirsch   161

Acknowledgments   165

Appendix: Beyond a Building: Tracing the Impermanence of
      Sacred Spaces in the Biblical Narrative   167

Bibliography   175

Donor List   181

FOREWORD
Joseph W. Handley, Jr., PhD

Before I met Danny Sathyadass, I heard about him through the alum network of A3, a global movement committed to equipping and multiplying transformational leaders. As an alum of A3, Danny's name kept surfacing in conversations—spoken of with admiration, respect, and a deep sense of spiritual kinship. Those familiar with his ministry described a man marked by humility, innovation, and a profound dependence on Christ. When I met Danny in person, I quickly understood why so many people spoke so highly of him. His authenticity, love for the church, and commitment to raising up Christ-centered leaders were evident from our very first conversation.

A3's vision is to develop leaders who live in intimacy with Christ and lead from that place of rooted identity. Danny exemplifies that vision. He's the kind of leader who doesn't just strategize—he listens. He doesn't merely initiate—he cultivates. And he doesn't just mobilize others—he walks alongside them, forming teams that embody what it means to be the people of God in action.

This book is a reflection of that lived experience. It's not written from the ivory tower of theory but from the trenches of ministry—in coffee shops and boardrooms, church basements and open-air gatherings, quiet conversations and bold steps of faith. Danny's writing blends solid biblical discipleship with practical, field-tested insights.

It's equal parts encouragement and blueprint—a resource that doesn't just tell you what to do but shows you how to do it, all while keeping Christ at the center.

What I love most about *Spark Teams* is its simplicity and clarity. Danny doesn't overcomplicate things. Instead, he calls us back to the fundamentals of how Jesus made disciples: in small, intimate teams saturated in prayer, focused on mission, and shaped by community. These "TEAMS" as he calls them, have the potential to ignite change far beyond what any individual could accomplish alone.

This book is not just another manual on leadership or disciple-making. It's a field guide, born from three decades of ministry, laced with Scripture, soaked in prayer, and marked by perseverance. Danny writes not as a polished expert offering formulas but as a fellow pilgrim—someone who has wrestled, listened, adapted, and trusted.

His vision aligns deeply with our work at A3. We've long championed the power of small, Christ-centered cohorts—leaders journeying together, listening to God, and discerning their next steps in mission. Danny's framework expands that ethos across vocations—not only to pastors and church planters but also to leaders in the marketplace, education, social entrepreneurship, and beyond. Wherever you lead, *Spark Teams* offers a model that can serve you well.

Throughout the book, Danny shares compelling stories from real-life disciple-making movements, community initiatives, and marketplace ministries rooted in kingdom values. These aren't just illustrations—they're invitations. As you read, you'll begin to imagine how these principles might take shape in your context. Whether you're launching a new initiative, seeking to revitalize a team, or exploring how to disciple others more faithfully, you'll find in these pages both inspiration and practical next steps.

Danny reminds us that lasting change doesn't come from charismatic personalities or perfect programs. It comes through ordinary people who trust an extraordinary God. It comes from teams who choose faithfulness over fame, and presence over platform. It comes from the daily practices of prayer, listening, accountability, and mutual encouragement. In an age that idolizes independence and speed, *Spark Teams* invites us back to something ancient and enduring: the slow, relational, Spirit-led work of forming communities that embody the gospel.

Danny never loses sight of Christ's sufficiency. Again and again, he returns to the central truth: Fruitfulness in God's kingdom is not measured by crowds or numbers but by faithfulness to Jesus. He quotes Oswald Chambers: "Don't rejoice in successful service but rejoice because you are rightly related to Me."[1] That posture of humility and trust permeates every chapter.

I also appreciate Danny's honesty. He doesn't shy away from the realities of disciple-making. He names the spiritual, relational, and organizational challenges that can derail good intentions. Yet instead of retreating in the face of difficulty, he leans into those moments with wisdom—gleaned from mentors, forged in the fire of experience, and grounded in the Word of God. His posture throughout is one of deep humility and unshakable hope, pointing us again and again to the faithfulness of Christ and the power of the Holy Spirit.

I was struck by how closely Danny's approach mirrors the most fruitful movements I've seen across the globe. In places as diverse as Asia, Africa, and the Americas, the same pattern holds true: small teams, deeply connected to Jesus, committed to one another, and willing to multiply. There's something powerful and catalytic about a few people saying "yes" to God together. Danny captures that power—and gives us a way to enter into it.

If you're holding this book, chances are you're hungry. Hungry for a better way to lead. Hungry to see your faith community grow. Hungry for discipleship that's real and sustainable. Or maybe you're longing for transformation in your city, workplace, or family—and

---

[1]   Oswald Chambers, "Usefulness or Relationship?" *My Utmost For His Highest*, accessed September 15, 2022, https://utmost.org/usefulness-or-relationship/.

wondering how the gospel might take root there. Whatever your context, this book offers hope and direction.

For those of us in leadership—whether in the marketplace, ministry, or missions—*Spark Teams* brings both challenge and encouragement. The challenge is to reimagine leadership in ways that are relational, humble, and centered on Christ. The encouragement is this: When we do, the Spirit moves—often in surprising and beautiful ways.

To those weary from the weight of institutional models that feel distant from real life—this book is for you.

To those longing to see communities transformed from the inside out—this book is for you.

To those asking, "What can I really do with just a few faithful people?"—this book is for you.

I encourage you to read this book slowly, prayerfully, and with others. Don't just consume the content—let it shape you. Better yet, let it spark something in you. A conversation. A team. A new rhythm of prayer. A decision to invest in someone else's journey. You may be surprised by what God ignites through your simple "yes."

Spark Teams is more than a book. It's a field manual for kingdom impact. It's a call to return to the way of Jesus—and to walk that road with others. I'm grateful to Danny for putting this resource into the hands of leaders across the globe. And I'm hopeful for the sparks it will ignite—in churches, in workplaces, in neighborhoods, and in lives.

In my own leadership journey across global networks and local communities, I've come to believe this: True transformation begins not with strategy but with surrendered people. *Spark Teams* is a book for such people—those ready to live, lead, and serve with a surrendered heart and a team at their side.

Read it. Share it. Live it.

Let the spark begin.

INTRODUCTION

On the streets of urban Bangalore, where I grew up, numerous small stores displayed makeshift signs advertising Xerox copies for as little as forty paisa to one rupee (less than 0.012 USD) per page. I don't recall ever seeing slick billboards or magazine advertisements for Xerox photocopy machines, but these simple Xerox signs made me associate the name Xerox exclusively with photocopying. It wasn't until much later, during an Indian train journey, that I learned from an enthusiastic Xerox marketing executive that Xerox was actually a company. He proudly explained that one of the primary reasons for Xerox's success was their branding strategy, which made the name synonymous with photocopying—similar to how "Google" has come to mean a web search. However, this very strategy ultimately contributed to Xerox's downfall.

Michael Hiltzik, a columnist for the *Los Angeles Times*, wrote: "The copier was probably the most successful industrial product of its time ... Xerox's entire being was geared toward building and exploiting the copier."[1] In the late 1970s, Xerox built Palo Alto Research Center (PARC) and employed energetic intellectuals with a mandate to create a new world. At one point, 58 percent of the world's top one hundred computer researchers were employed at PARC. Former PARC researchers John Warnock and Larry Tessler testify

---

[1]   Nathaniel Meyersohn, "How Xerox Became a Verb," CNN Business, February 2, 2018.

that they were given total intellectual freedom.[2] These talented young researchers eventually invented groundbreaking technologies that we take for granted today, such as Ethernet, a prototype of the personal computer, a commercial version of the mouse, and laser printers. But Xerox management's obsession with photocopiers blinded them to the immense potential of computers and hindered the validation of the researchers' creative efforts.

Meanwhile, a twenty-four-year-old college dropout observed a demonstration of these innovations at PARC, and, after ten minutes, realized their world-changing potential. This dropout was none other than Steve Jobs of Apple, who went on to market much of PARC's inventions. Jobs stated, "They were basically copier heads, they just had no clue about a computer and what it could do, and so they grabbed defeat from the greatest victory in the computer industry. Xerox could have owned the entire computer industry. It could have been … a company ten times its size."[3]

We could say this scenario is reflective of the church. Just as Xerox became synonymous with photocopying, the church has sadly become synonymous with buildings and infrastructure. Consider how the word "church" is used today:

- "What church do you go to?" (referring to an institution or organization)
- "What time does church start?" (referring to an event)
- "Look at that beautiful old church." (referring to a building)[4]

Through our language and practices, we have unintentionally

---

2   ZDNet, "PARC Scientist Recalls Jobs' Famous Xerox Visits," YouTube, November 11, 2011, https://www.youtube.com/watch?v=ZOF-j6Nxm04.

3   Ringo Pebam, "How Steve Jobs Got the Ideas of GUI from XEROX," YouTube, January 4, 2014, https://www.youtube.com/watch?v=J33pVRdxWbw.

4   Richard Jacobson, "What Constitutes a Real church?" YouTube, October 17, 2013, https://www.youtube.com/watch?v=ZGmeIUK4xpE.

confined the concept of church to a location for just a few hours a week. Just as Xerox executives failed to recognize the latent potential within PARC, we have overlooked the awesome resurrection power that has always been within us. We need to look beyond the four walls, beyond specific times and locations, and rebrand ourselves to reflect who we truly are.

Many books go to great lengths to provide clarity on the church, but my focus in these pages is to emphasize that the church is essentially a community of Christ's disciples who mutually edify one another. Buildings—regardless of size and including homes—are merely structures to facilitate community. The size of the group or infrastructure are secondary. What is most vital is that disciples acknowledge Christ as their head and willingly and wholeheartedly follow him.

The Gameplan Huddle

To effectively embody our identity as a community of Christ's disciples, we must embrace our role as active participants in his mission. Like a team on the field, this requires coming together in unity. In any team sport, amid the crowd, the noise, the distractions, and attractions on all fronts, players often come together in a close huddle with arms around each other's shoulders. They lean in to ensure they pay close attention to one another, discussing plays, re-strategizing, making corrections, or giving a victory cry—all within a matter of seconds. This huddle is not a prolonged coaching session that covers the details of specific skills or plays; rather, it consists of a short phrase or hand signal to ensure everyone is aligned on the "secret" plan.

The game plan huddle has become a common feature in many sports. It's not meant for scholars, spectators, or commentators. Instead, it's a quick gathering of the actual players on the field who are actively engaged in the game.

The metaphor of a game plan huddle represents the focus of

this book. It's intended for those eager to participate in the game or those already on the field engaged in disciple-making. It's for those who know the challenges and realities of serving. This book is not for scholars, spectators, or commentators but for those eager to be practitioners—those focused on action.

The approach I suggest will be helpful if you are a bi-vocational disciple-maker actively serving in your community. You may not have the time or resources to track ministry growth or to serve as a ministry leader in a national or international ministry. This book will also be useful if you are a trainer or leader, because of the emphasis on facilitating change from the ground up. The themes discussed will be brief, assuming that many of these fundamental truths have already been addressed. Although most of us do not struggle with our convictions about discipleship, the problem often lies in the consistency of practice. Therefore, this book aims to present various disciple-making principles in a practical format to inspire you to stay the course and continue moving forward.

My Journey Toward Disciple-Making

In the early 2000s, call centers mushroomed in and around the city of Bangalore, India. Young people who joined these multinational companies earned more money than their parents. With newfound wealth and independence, many strayed into a reckless lifestyle, quite contrary to that of their conservative, religious parents of varying faiths. Working late nights to cater to primarily American or British companies led to significant relationship problems between spouses and within families. Some church youth groups simply disbanded because young people were either working or partying on Saturday nights. News reporters and preachers alike referred to the disintegration of values across society.

After gathering with those from our church involved in call centers, we recognized the urgent need to reach out to this community, understanding that this trend would likely stay.

In 2005, we moved to Whitefield (a neighborhood of Bangalore) to pioneer a church, trusting God to provide for us. I remember walking around Ulsoor Lake, wondering whether I was putting my wife and three sons (ranging in age from six months to seven years) through unnecessary challenges. My wife and I were concerned about our children's education, as there were hardly any good schools in the area at that time. I also worried about housing costs, as rent prices were skyrocketing. However, numerous miracles of God's providence confirmed our call to serve in that place; and we began our journey with a sense of adventure, alongside our friends Jeff Imam and Jonathan Sikha. In January 2005, a handful of us started meeting as a church. Having read Rick Warren's *Purpose Driven Church*, I envisioned us becoming an urban international megachurch.[5] Yet, for two whole years, our attendance hovered around a dozen. Jeff Imam faithfully attended our gatherings but fell sound asleep every Sunday in his favorite corner, after working all night at a call center.

I began to wonder whether we should hold multiple services on Sunday or perhaps throughout the week. During this time, I learned about young people gathering for prayer—in office cubicles, garage basements, or homes—at midnight or 4 a.m., or other odd hours. I was often awakened at 4 a.m. on Saturday mornings by the sounds of Christian worship from a neighbor's home. Young people from a call center had chosen to worship and study Scripture together after their shift. I wondered why this form of church, taking place where life happens and coordinated by young people, could not be considered authentic. I noticed that some of the young people felt guilty, either because they couldn't attend their local church with their family or because their parents or other church members criticized them for being worldly.

Inspired by stories about the house churches of China and

---

[5]   Rick Warren, *The Purpose Driven Church: Every Church Is Big in God's Eyes* (Grand Rapids, MI: Zondervan, 1995).

the gatherings described in the book of Acts, I was prompted to read further and seek out people engaged in this form of ministry. A timely seminar offered by author and Christian movements researcher David Garrison and team, along with personal mentoring from Neill Mims in church planting, set me on a path of discovery. We transitioned our church gathering to a home-church model and experienced phenomenal growth, especially when serving as catalysts—even while I pursued a master's degree through the University of Wales in association with TAFTEE (The Association for Theological Education by Extension) and conducted doctoral research at SAIACS (South Asia Institute of Advanced Christian Studies).

The Meaning of Church

My studies and connections led me to delve deeper into the meaning of church. The early church's practice of connecting individual believers together reflected Christ's example of forming a tight-knit community with the Twelve. Before his ascension, Christ led, inspired, and trained them, which "involved His own constant personal association with a few chosen men."[6] After the Holy Spirit was poured out at Pentecost, the apostles equipped believers in homes or the temple courts by teaching and praying for them, while the people mutually edified one another. "It was the church that was the means for the follow-up of all those who decided to recognize Jesus as Lord. That is, the group of believers became the body of Christ, and as such ministered to each other and collectively."[7] The New Testament always referred to the church as the *people* of God; it was never about a *place*. Disciple-making was *everyone's* responsibility. Every member had a role to play, as part of the body of

---

6   Robert E. Coleman, *The Master Plan of Evangelism* (Old Tappan, NJ: Revell, 1963), 46.

7   Coleman, *The Master Plan of Evangelism*, 46.

Christ—the church. Therefore, church is not where you go for a service but about Christ's people who serve, wherever they go. It is about making disciples and being the church, wherever life happens.

In the New Testament, all members were expected and encouraged to participate and "spur one another toward love and good deeds" (Heb. 10:24). The church was primarily made up of vibrant small groups of disciples within a particular region who often gathered in homes and were actively involved in one another's lives (Acts 2:42–46). These gatherings facilitated fellowship and discipleship. Ordinary people generally welcomed Jesus or the early apostles into their homes (Matt. 9:10–11; Acts 2:46–47), but the temple and synagogue authorities often resisted and rejected Jesus, his message, and his followers (John 1:11–12; Acts 4:1–3). Though large gatherings of the believing community did occur in the temple courts, this did not last for long; the religious leaders eventually succeeded in launching a great persecution against the church, prompting the believers to flee from Jerusalem (Acts 8:1–3).

Initially, my research into the function of home churches convinced me that this was the approach to take, particularly for the evolving context of India. However, a poignant encounter challenged my assumptions. Following a training session on home churches, a Hindu background believer expressed her deep concern. She asked how it was possible for her to open her home when there were threats of attack from her entire village community. In a community-oriented society such as India—and especially in an Indian village setting—matters of marriage, livelihood, and faith are not merely private affairs. The communal nature of Indian society meant that her choice to follow Christ would inevitably draw the attention and potential hostility of her entire community. She shared stories of other Christians from neighboring villages who had been beaten or ostracized from their community. For her, attending a larger, more anonymous church in a neighboring town seemed like a better idea. I realized that I had to rethink how I articulated the meaning of "church." By focusing on the term "home church," I was still inadvertently placing undue emphasis on a building. It was then that I intentionally began to focus on the need to foster discipleship *principles* to help strengthen believers in their commitment to Christ and to one another—in other words, to emphasize *functions* that aid disciple-making rather than *forms* (such as buildings) that aid or support the gathering.

Learning Through Experimenting

As we began to see growth in our Indian context, we also saw how serving as catalysts sparked exponential multiplication of churches, well beyond our circles of influence. Here are a few examples.

- **Trans World Radio India (TWR)** initiated over seventeen thousand Radio Homes spoken in more than seventy Indian languages. (A Radio Home is a small group of five or six members who fellowship and learn together by listening to radio messages stored on secure digital cards.) Conversations I had with the director of TWR eventually led to the formation of Radio Homes. This idea has since spread to neighboring countries.

- **Chandan Sah,** inspired by the simplicity of how we gathered, founded Empower Bihar, which initiated thousands of home fellowships/disciple-making-movement groups. It has since grown well beyond Bihar.

- **Srinivas** started **Jeevo Daya** and has a network of home churches among the Kannada-speaking people in Hoskote, Bangalore.

These encouraging results, although significant, should not serve as the sole determinant for choosing a particular methodology. Our journey has revealed a much more nuanced reality. We have not seen favorable results across all contexts or among all people groups. We faced resistance; and some individuals became preoccupied with their own lives, causing the ministry to stagnate or reach a standstill. We also recognize how our own inadequacies and shortcomings contributed to this standstill. We cannot boast of exponential growth in numbers in the cities, though our efforts primarily focused there. For instance, we did not see rapid multiplication in Bangalore or Dallas, where we had relocated to serve among the Indian diasporas. Although we did see *some* phenomenal results, they were primarily limited to rural areas. The past twenty years have been filled with hurdles, loneliness, and tearful prayers. The challenges often felt more intense because those of us eager to serve worked closely with each other. The practical and adaptable framework offered in this book, therefore, comes not from theory but from hard-won, realistic, and experiential understanding, bearing the marks of real struggles and the strength of the insights gained through them.

It's Not About Numbers or Methods

The principles in this book are not intended to be a formula for exponential growth. Instead, my deepest hope is to encourage disciple-makers and church planters to cultivate a vibrant and sustained relationship with the Savior, particularly those not seeing significant numerical growth. Repentance, salvation, and the building of Christ's body, the church, are ultimately in God's hands. His promise in John 15:16, however, assures us that those who abide in him will "bear fruit—fruit that will last," which may not necessarily be visible in our lifetime. A case in point is Jesus himself: After three years of intense supernatural deliverance ministry and authoritative preaching throughout the region, only 120 followers gathered in the upper room. Oswald Chambers, commenting on Luke 10:20 ("Do not rejoice that the spirits submit to you, but rejoice that your names are written in heaven"), highlights the futility of evaluating ministry effectiveness based on results, urging us instead to celebrate a right relationship with God.

He writes, "Don't rejoice in successful service but rejoice because you are rightly related to [God]."[8]

We often tend to gravitate toward methods at the expense of prayer and hearing God. Several years into ministry, I realized I was working *for* God but not *with* him. I know of friends who have experienced the same. Maybe you feel similarly. This book, therefore, emphasizes the need to work with God by listening to his voice. I was profoundly impacted by some training on home churches that I received from Tony and Felicity Dale, who pioneered a house church movement in the UK and the US and who authored several books on the same theme. They highlighted the importance of hearing God, and this emphasis has left an indelible mark on me, particularly having observed and experienced situations where minor differences in a process or a method sadly became the reason for organizations or people to part ways. I felt liberated by understanding how to hear and apply God's direction in a specific context without having to rigidly follow a particular approach. The necessity of hearing and following God's leading is a consistent theme throughout these pages.

Overview of the Book

This book offers practical guidance for obedient teams of disciples to function as the church, bringing transformation wherever they are. It shows that church can be a growing revolutionary movement of multiple, autonomous yet interdependent Christ-centered teams. It need not be limited to a static monument or a hierarchical infrastructure. My goal is not to discount or compare megachurches with traditional churches, or even home churches for that matter. My aim, rather, is to highlight the significance of committed teams of disciples as agents of change.

To explore this concept, this book is structured in two parts:

---

8   Chambers, "Usefulness or Relationship?"

Part one explores God's foundational initiative of love, which is evident in his relationship with the people of Israel and through Jesus' relationship with the early disciples. God's approach is encapsulated by the terms *draw, influence,* and *empower* (forming the acronym DIE), highlighting the overarching theme of God's love personified in Christ's selfless sacrifice for the church.

Part two emphasizes our responsibilities as integral members of God's family, the church. It highlights how Christ's power at work within us equips us to wholeheartedly engage in key functions that help us mature and stay healthy as his church. These vital functions—*teaching, evangelism, adoration, mentoring,* and *sharing*—form the acronym TEAMS. A healthy team, characterized by these elements, has the innate capacity to reproduce Christ-centered teams. Rather than offering a standardized method, this book highlights flexible principles that anyone can apply in response to the Holy Spirit's prompting, especially within the context of a team. It emphasizes the brilliant simplicity of Christ's approach, who accommodated creativity and diversity to connect with various cultural contexts.

While this book can be read individually, it would be highly beneficial if teams read it together to facilitate discussion. The verses at the end of the chapters reinforce the themes highlighted. Teams that practice these principles can gain an experiential understanding of how disciple-making and being church take place through their collective effort as a team.

Throughout this book, you will encounter the inspiring stories of many unsung heroes who applied these principles in different contexts. I hope they will encourage you to stay the course as a disciple-maker. Notably, most of these stories feature individuals from diverse faith backgrounds in India who do not have a Christian or Western worldview. I have intentionally included these stories to highlight the complexity of cultures and the varying backgrounds they bring, a reality reflected in many of today's global cities. My aim is to emphasize the need to truly listen to the Spirit of God and invest time to understand particular individuals or people groups, rather than merely adopting ready-made approaches.

Just as the Xerox executives were blinded by their success with copiers and thus failed to grasp the revolutionary potential of personal computers, we in the church have often limited our vision to brick-and-mortar spaces. We need the presence of Christ embodied through his disciples to permeate society in street corners, coffee shops, prisons, government offices, and business centers. The focus is not on how we can *do* church but how we can *be* the church, *wherever life happens.* Like the early disciples who grew to love and serve Christ, teams of believers can be the church, bringing hope and light to any context, even in the most hostile and challenging environments.

May this book be an inspiration and a source of guidance to spark Christ-centered teams to be channels of God's mercy. May the Lord enable you to lovingly serve and share the gospel of grace to those who are hurting, confident in God's power to bring transformation.

May our Lord Jesus Christ himself and God our Father, who loved us and by his grace gave us eternal encouragement and good hope, encourage your hearts and strengthen you in every good deed and word.

2 THESSALONIANS 2:16–17

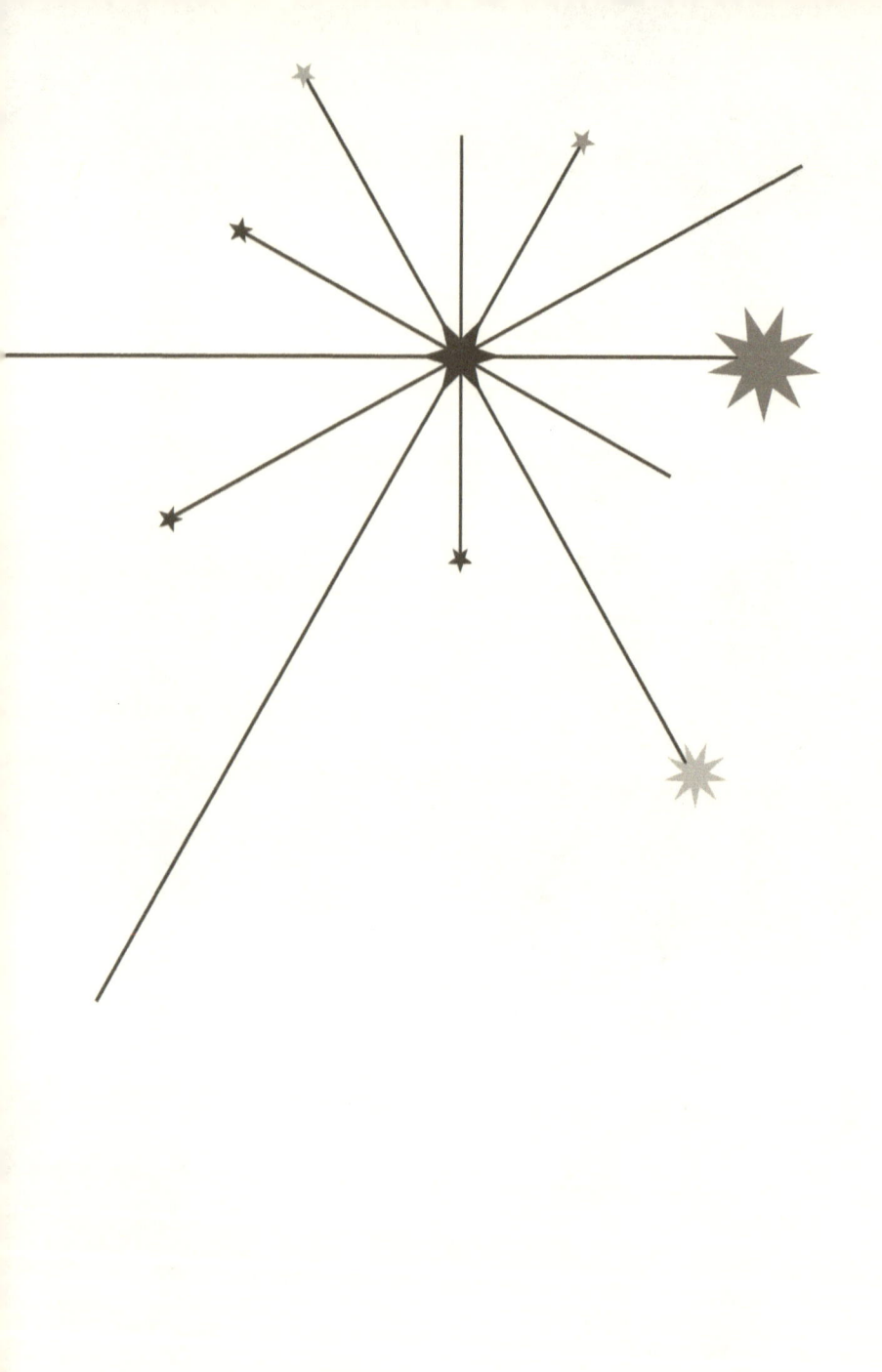

PART ONE

DIE

God's Initiative of Love

I used to think following Christ was all about the promise of abundant life here and eternal life hereafter; but I gradually came to understand the weight of responsibility of daily dying to self.

PART ONE EXPLORES the foundational principles of discipleship and disciple-making, emphasizing God's initiative of love through the framework of draw, influence, and empower (DIE). Without a firm grasp of DIE, the principles of TEAMS (teaching, evangelism, adoration, mentoring, and sharing) explored in part two risk becoming a set of disconnected activities or a human-centered program rather than a Spirit-led journey of disciple-making. Therefore, before diving into the practicalities of TEAMS, it is crucial to deeply understand and internalize the foundational truth that discipleship is rooted in God's loving initiative (draw), nurtured through authentic example (influence), and aimed at releasing others into their full potential in Christ (empower). This foundational understanding will infuse the application of TEAMS with purpose, authenticity, and lasting impact.

This section highlights Christ's exemplary sacrifice and service, culminating in his sacrifice on the cross to offer hope and life to all. We love and serve him only because he first loved us. The following chapters aim to illuminate the high standard Christ set for us, serving as our example as we engage in disciple-making through the foundations of drawing, influencing, and empowering.

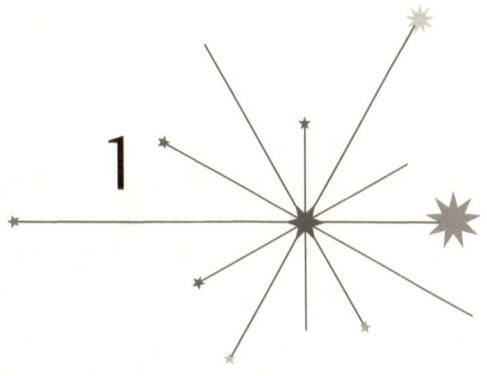

GIVE UP, TAKE UP, AND KEEP UP THE CROSS OF JESUS

I used to think serving God was all about my abilities, but I've come to realize it's really about my availability.

ON MY FIRST day at the Word of Life Bible Institute, I found myself walking alone by the serene waters of Schroon Lake, in upstate New York. As a twenty-three-year-old, I was overwhelmed with gratitude that the Lord had brought me all the way from Bangalore, with a full scholarship and all expenses paid during my course of study. I was also grateful that I had gotten engaged to Sayo, my wife-to-be, just two days before I left.

Intending to focus my studies on Christian music, I was thrilled to be at Word of Life, as it offered a gateway to pursue a career in music. I had high hopes and a head full of dreams, eager to attempt great things for God—or so I thought. Almost immediately, I heard a voice within my heart: "Would you be willing to sacrifice your guitar and go anywhere, even if people do not recognize your musical abilities?" Suddenly, my thoughts of sublime adoration were barraged with conflicting thoughts, as an image of a guitar on the altar was embedded in my mind. How could God ask me to do such a thing? After all, I knew it was a gift he had given me. But this thought, which came like a bolt from the blue, seemed entirely contrary to what I had envisioned. I couldn't fathom how I could say yes to this gentle nudge, even if it was from God. After a few minutes of resisting, I reluctantly agreed.

It wasn't until later that evening that I became sure this prompting was indeed of God. Harry Bollback, who at the time was vice president of Word of Life, was the speaker at the mission's conference. He shared his experience of serving among tribal people in South America. What caught my attention was that although he was a successful musician, he had chosen to sacrifice his music career. There I was, being challenged by someone who was content and purposeful, even though he had given up his dream in order to follow Christ's call. Toward the end of the service, I responded to the ministry invitation by walking up to the front and throwing a stick into the fire, symbolically declaring my allegiance to follow God's plan and relinquish my own idea of service to God.

I was excited to write and share about this life-changing decision with Christian friends and family, but when the year was done and I prepared to leave the US, the thought that a career in music might never materialize hit me hard. On arriving in Bangalore, my frustration grew even further, as I applied for various jobs and encountered one closed door after another. After weeks of disappointment, I discovered the journal entry I had made more than a year earlier, saying I was willing to do anything, even if people didn't recognize my musical abilities. At that moment, I realized how easily I had returned to my earlier pursuit; I had limited my search to jobs that would guarantee a platform to showcase my musical abilities. I had to confess and surrender once again. I wrote the following song after hearing a message from Chris Gnanakan, who was serving as a pastor in Bangalore.

I'm tired of chasing those pretty rainbows,
Tired of spinning round and round.
There lie the shattered dreams of my life,
And at the feet of Jesus, I lay them down.

I now give up, to take up and keep up the cross of my Jesus.
I now give up, to take up and keep up the cross of my Lord.
I'm not a fool to give up what I can't keep, to gain what I cannot lose.

I'm tired of fishing on the seas of ambition,
Tired of pulling strings my own way.
There lies my catch: only weeds of confusion.
O Lord, your voice I hear; I will now obey.[1]

It was on giving up my aspirations for a platform that the Lord unexpectedly opened the door to serve alongside my wife at Banaswadi Bible Church in the outskirts of Bangalore, under the guidance of Pastor Chris Gnanakan. Pioneering in this environment, far from the spotlight I once craved, proved to be a foundational crucible for our family, preparing us for the journey ahead. It was a safe haven for my wife and me to mature in our relationship within a close-knit community of believers. In that unassuming space, we saw much fruit; and several children, young people, and families devoted themselves to Christ. The joys and hardships of ministry forged within us an unshakable reliance on God, providing the impetus needed to eventually take bolder steps of faith. Our experience mirrored a significant biblical pattern: God often calls us to count the cost *before* commissioning us for service. The Seventy-Two (Luke 10) were commissioned *after* Jesus had navigated a series of encounters that starkly illuminated the radical demands of following him, including

---

[1] "I Now Give Up," by Danny Sathyadass, produced by BandLab Singapore Pte Ltd, ReverbNation, November 2010, https://www.reverbnation.com/dannysathyadass/song/2788756-i-now-give-up.

even surrendering worthwhile genuine concerns, such as secure housing and taking care of parents (Luke 9:57–62).

Christ's call to represent him for a cause demands our lives, our all; it's about leaving all to follow him, just as the twelve disciples did in the Gospels. Jesus said,

> Very truly I tell you, unless a kernel of wheat falls to the ground and dies, it remains only a single seed. But if it dies, it produces many seeds. Anyone who loves their life will lose it, while anyone who hates their life in this world will keep it for eternal life. Whoever serves me must follow me; and where I am, my servant also will be. My Father will honor the one who serves me.
>
> JOHN 12:24–26

The Cost of Being a Disciple

The first call of a disciple is to die to self. Jesus repeatedly expressed and embodied the cost of dying to self and surrendering to God's will. For example, after feeding the five thousand, the crowd intended to forcibly make Jesus their king (John 6:15). Jesus could have easily christened the solitary place as a miracle mountain or ashram and used his popularity for his own gains or even to recruit more disciples to serve on his "pastoral team" so they could "minister" to the crowds. However, he chose to send his disciples ahead of him, while he lingered on to disperse the crowds before going by himself to a solitary place to pray (Matt. 14:22–24).

Later that night, the twelve disciples found themselves on a stormy sea, straining at the oars. Jesus eventually walked on the water toward them and encouraged Peter to do the same. However, the life of a disciple is not always marked by miraculous walks on water. More often, it resembles the Twelve straining at the oars on a stormy sea. It is in this steadfast commitment—even amid the struggle, even where there seems to be no answer—that we demonstrate our willingness to follow Jesus. Sometimes our willingness to follow will involve stepping out of the boat; other times, it will require persisting in rowing.

Shortly after the calming of the storm, Christ confronted the crowd about their false motives in following him. This difficult challenge prompted many to withdraw from him. Jesus even asked the Twelve if they also wanted to leave (John 6:60–66). His popularity had dropped considerably by the time he finished this discourse. Yet Jesus continually chose to follow the Father's will, even when it made him unpopular, and even when it eventually cost him his life.

As leaders, it's easy for us to get drawn into people-pleasing by falling into an endless cycle of ministry activities. The crowds often viewed Jesus as merely a miracle-worker and promise-keeper—a sentiment echoed in our contemporary worship—but not as a disciple-maker. Many of our "Christian" endeavors revolve around perpetually feeding and entertaining crowds, with those of us who minister—or "perform"—deriving a false sense of worth and basking in the limelight of accolades from the masses. But by doing so, we neglect the few disciples God has called us to lead. Whether we are new believers or experienced ministry leaders, Christ's discernment is absolutely essential to disperse crowds or even discontinue some of those "mountain top" activities and instead die to self and focus on what the Father desires. We need to follow Christ's example and spend time alone with the Father and then associate ourselves closely with the few he has called us to lead, who are likely straining at the oars on a stormy sea.

You may have seen images of wives and children bidding farewell to courageous husbands and fathers during times of war. Many of these men went on to suffer immensely or even lost their lives in battle, as they attempted to defend their country. This is the kind of commitment Christ is looking for in his disciples; those who will take up his cross and follow him (Luke 9:23). Bonhoeffer reiterates this call in his book *The Cost of Discipleship*: "When Christ calls a man, he bids him come and die."[2]

---

[2]   Dietrich Bonhoeffer, *The Cost of Discipleship* (London: SCM Press Ltd, 1989), 89, 90.

DIE: Jesus' Way to Change Lives

In this section we will explore what it means to DIE—draw, influence, and empower—highlighting three key ways God initiates love and transforms his people.

This exploration of DIE isn't merely a framework for effective discipleship and disciple-making; it's a reflection of the Christian concept of "death to self." Just as Christ humbled himself, taking on human form, and ultimately dying on the cross, so too must we die to our own self-centered desires and ambitions if we are to truly follow him and participate in his transformative work. It is in surrendering our own agendas, our need for control, and our desire for self-promotion that we become vessels through which God can truly draw others to himself (John 12:32), influence their growth (Gal. 2:20), and empower them for service (Acts 1:8). This "death" is a realignment of our will with God's, allowing his love to flow through us unhindered, transforming us and equipping us to transform others. In this posture of humility and surrender we discover the true power of DIE, mirroring Christ's own path of sacrifice and service.

DIE: How God Transforms Us

Before we can disciple others, we must first be active disciples ourselves. Thus, we must first engage with the transformation Christ longs to bring in our own lives. The lens of draw, influence, and empower helps us understand how God initiates his transformation in us.

Draw: God takes the first step toward humans by showering us with his love and meeting our needs in tangible and unique ways. He has ultimately done this through the gift of his son, Jesus. God came to earth through the person of Christ and associated himself with humans, in our pain and suffering. The journey toward God can be sparked by various means, including signs, wonders, and various supernatural events, as well as God's Word, Spirit, the created world, and the authentic witness of Christians. Whereas most other faiths tend to incite fear to obtain people's allegiance, God, who is rich in mercy, draws people to himself in love.

Influence: Rather than imposing his reign, God graciously influences those who have been drawn to him, like a gentle shepherd or a loving father who invests time with his child. God's gentle leadership means he does not forcibly impose his rule but instead pursues us with love.

Empower: After we are drawn to God and influenced by his love and guidance, the Lord empowers us to serve him and to partner with him in his work. God endows us with his gifts and power. He desires fellowship and intimacy, not servitude; he blesses his people with every spiritual blessing in Christ.

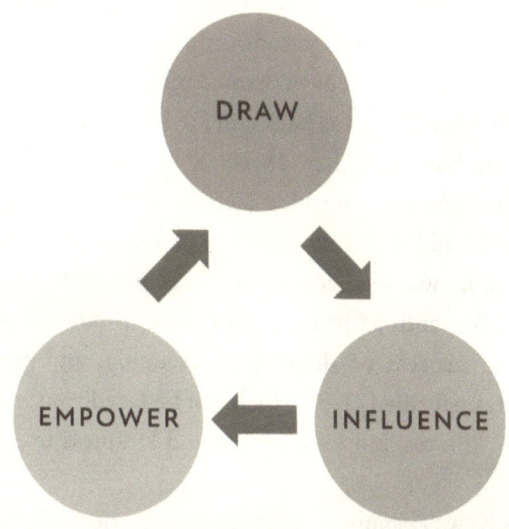

DIE: Partnering with God in Disciple-Making

Many leaders dictate, drive, and lord it over their people. But when we adopt Christ's process of drawing, influencing, and empowering, we partner with God for his transformation.

As we seek to *draw* people to Christ, we focus on God's initiative of love and grace in attracting people, rather than relying on fear or coercion. We aim to *influence* them by being Christlike in our example, nurturing and guiding those who have been drawn to God, and helping them grow in their faith and become more like Christ. This involves investing time in their lives, offering gentle guidance, and helping them to take ownership of their faith journey. And we *empower* others to worship and serve with Christ by recognizing and affirming their gifts and providing opportunities to use those gifts for ministry.

DIE as a Cyclical Process in the Biblical Narrative

Throughout the Bible, we can see how the elements of DIE occur cyclically. Consider Jacob, whose deceitful nature was undeniable. When he had reached rock bottom—alone in the desert and fleeing Esau's wrath—God could have shamed him. Instead, God *drew* him with a vision of angels going back and forth to heaven and reassured him with his blessing (Gen. 28:10–22). Despite Laban's deceit, God's gracious *influence* enabled Jacob's success through blessing, wisdom, and fulfilled promises. When he left to return to the land of his father, he was well equipped and *empowered* with livestock, wealth, family, and additional men who provided protection. This cyclical process of drawing, influencing, and empowering eventually transformed Jacob. No doubt he faced consequences for many of his failures, but God's grace and kindness overshadowed them all.

In the New Testament, after his resurrection, Christ *drew* to himself all the disciples who had deserted him (John 21) He appeared on the shore while they were fishing at dawn, and once again *influenced* them with his presence and his miraculous power. He *empowered* them to catch fish, which they had been unable to do all night. When they reached the shore, Christ did not shame or insult them with an "I told you so" speech. Instead, he *drew* them to himself, demonstrating love by preparing a barbeque breakfast on the beach. Like a gentle shepherd, he then *influenced* Peter, by asking him three times if he truly loved him—mirroring the three times Peter denied him. Assured of Peter's love and commitment, Christ *empowered* Peter with greater responsibility of feeding his sheep (John 21:15–25). A few days later, Peter demonstrated this empowerment by courageously addressing a crowd near to the area where he had denied Christ. We read that the religious leaders took note that Peter and John had indeed been with Jesus (Acts 4:13).

Combining DIE in Disciple-Making

When applying draw, influence and empower to disciple-making, it can be viewed not only as a linear or cyclical process but also as a combination of all three aspects, where different proportions will be required according to the person and their faith journey. Visualizing the various frequencies of a sound console may help to grasp this concept: A skilled sound technician adjusts various frequencies such as lows, mids, and highs to obtain the desired sound, while also taking into consideration factors such as the type of building, the type of instruments, and the number of people present in the audience. Likewise, in our disciple-making, we will adjust the aspects of *draw, influence,* and *empower,* depending on the personality and background of the person or their season of life. It's a unique blend of all three. The bar graph on the following page shows how this might play out.

A young believer may need more acts of kindness to experience God, while a mature believer may need more opportunities to take on responsibility, to exercise what he or she has already been empowered with. Since each individual and group is unique, disciple-makers need to exercise wisdom and pay close attention to the Lord's direction, rather than imposing a standard linear or cyclical process. Disciples are not mass produced, as the following examples illustrate.

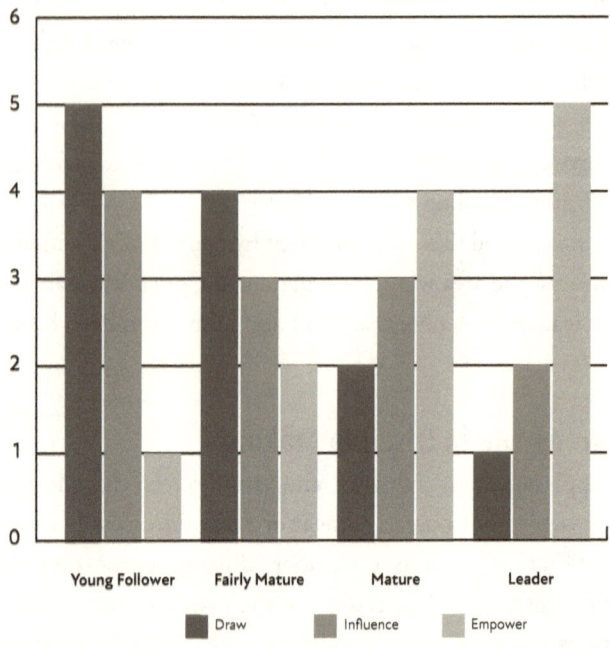

Through various God-orchestrated events, God led my wife and me to interact with a young couple. As we got to know them, we found out that the wife had been sexually abused as a child, and the husband had been brought up by a physically violent father and an emotionally hostile mother. It wasn't until two years of consistently meeting with them that we discovered how volatile their family life was, and that they were on the verge of going their separate ways. We found ourselves needing to offer pastoral care even though we would have preferred to spend our time investing in the multiplication of churches. Praise God, he eventually healed their marriage and opened doors for the husband to become a discipleship coach on a national level. He later started multiple initiatives and churches. In this scenario, God seemed to first direct and focus our energies on drawing and influencing them with love. We only minimally and gradually empowered them with concepts related to church and discipleship at this stage. Once healing had taken place, the focus could shift to empowering them.

In contrast to the above-mentioned experience, just a few conversations with the CEO of Trans World Radio India resulted in phenomenal growth. I shared insights on discipleship and movement principles and, as a well-established leader, he quickly grasped the concepts and creatively initiated thousands of discipleship groups across the country. In this situation, my involvement was more catalytic, focused on highlighting practical principles that related to empowering. The aspects of drawing or influencing were minuscule.

Embracing the Call to DIE

Jim Elliot, who died as a martyr when attempting to contact the Huaorani tribe in 1956, wrote less than seven years earlier, "He is no fool who gives what he cannot keep to gain that which he cannot lose."[3] Two years after Jim's death, his widow, Elizabeth Elliot, returned to serve among the people who had killed her husband. Their exemplary service and ministry have not only transformed lives in Ecuador but have also inspired many around the world to serve Christ, despite difficult and life-threatening situations.

Martyrs do not arrive at such conclusions in haste. It involves years of communing and partnering with Christ by allowing him to draw, influence, and empower them. By engaging in quiet meditation, revelation, prayer, and obedience in the little tasks, martyrs can take daring steps or make bold declarations of their allegiance to Christ. Similarly, the apostle Paul's effectiveness as a servant of the gospel cannot be attributed to merely his determined effort to move from place to place but rather to the revelation he received (Gal. 1:12, 16). We know very little of Jesus' life for the first thirty years—we might call these his silent years—and we know he spent many hours alone in prayer during his three years of ministry. Empowerment from God for effective and lasting service only comes by first allowing him to draw

---

[3] Kevin Halloran, "Jim Elliot's Journal Entry with 'He Is No Fool...' Quote," Anchored in Christ, October 28, 2013, https://www.kevinhalloran.net/jim-elliot-quote-he-is-no-fool/.

and influence us. To do this, we need to incorporate intentional times of solitude with him. If we are eager to serve as disciple-makers, we cannot circumvent the need to be disciples ourselves. Knowing Christ and experiencing the magnitude of his love is key to bearing fruit that will last.

In the following three chapters, we will explore what it means to deeply engage with each of the DIE factors. We need to allow ourselves to be drawn to Christ in order for him to influence us by regularly connecting with him in prayer and through his Word—knowing who we are in him and understanding the depth of his love demonstrated in his finished work on the cross. Then, we can allow him to empower us—recognizing the gifts and the authority we have in him.

Try It Out

Below are a few practices to help you live out Christ's call to die to self.

- **Consider what the Lord is asking you to surrender to his purpose and plan:** Remember, this could mean giving up a noble pursuit. Rather than expecting him to put his seal of approval on your own list of dreams and desires, picture yourself approaching God with a blank sheet of paper with your name signed underneath. Trust him to write your job description for you.

- **Ask the Lord to help you persevere:** If you have been serving the Lord for a while, has the shallowness of God's people within the church or the resistance of people outside the fold made you weary? Remember, dying to self involves staying true to God's call, continuing to "row the boat" even when the storms blow against you. It's easier to stay motivated and enthusiastic when there are phenomenal results, but it takes a lot more faith and tenacity to stay true to God's call when things are difficult. Ask the Lord to help you stay on course.

- **Evaluate yourself in light of Christ's expression of DIE:** Have you found yourself being demanding and dictating orders, as a disciple-maker of your own children or the people God has entrusted you with? Have you found yourself insulting and intimidating them into submission? Or have you embarrassed them or exposed their sin so that you can enforce the right behavior or obtain results? Evaluate yourself in the light of Christ's humble way of drawing, influencing, and empowering people. Confess and seek the Lord to reaffirm his way, even as you read this book.

Meditate and Discuss

Reflect on what the following verses reveal about dying to self.

- "Whoever wants to be my disciple must deny themselves and take up their cross and follow me" (Mark 8:34).
- "We have left everything to follow you!" (Mark 10:28).
- "Those of you who do not give up everything you have cannot be my disciples" (Luke 14:33).
- "For God so loved the world that he gave his one and only Son, that whoever believes in him shall not perish but have eternal life" (John 3:16).
- "I have been crucified with Christ and I no longer live, but Christ lives in me" (Gal. 2:20).
- "I want to know Christ—yes, to know the power of his resurrection and participation in his sufferings, becoming like him in his death, and so, somehow, attaining to the resurrection from the dead" (Phil. 3:10–11).
- "Blessed is the one who perseveres under trial because, having stood the test, that person will receive the crown of life that the Lord has promised to those who love him" (James 1:12).

- "'He himself bore our sins' in his body on the cross, so that we might die to sins and live for righteousness; 'by his wounds you have been healed'" (1 Pet. 2:24).
- "This is how we know what love is: Jesus Christ laid down his life for us. And we ought to lay down our lives for our brothers and sisters" (1 John 3:16).

 *Any Questions?*

 *Any Ideas?*

 *Anything That Touches Your Heart?*

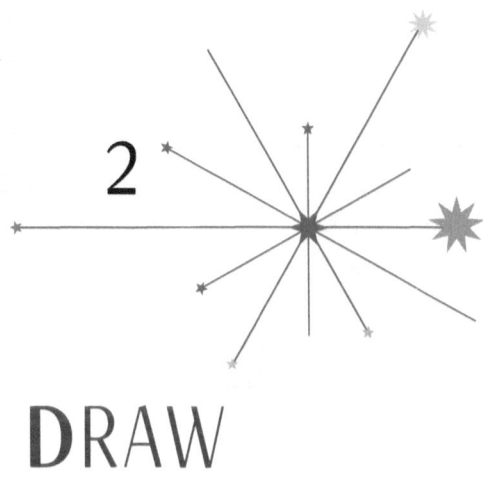

DRAW

I used to think successful endeavors were led by strong-willed directors who enforced goals, values, or purpose. But now I see that success from God's perspective involves people of character who sacrificially serve because God's love and kindness draws them.

MANY WHO GREW up in Indian schools prior to the 1980s likely recall playing school and holding sticks, imitating the teachers who often carried bamboo canes or wooden rulers to maintain classroom discipline. Some may also remember or have heard of teachers throwing heavy dusters. (These dusters were made of a wooden block with a soft, felt-like material attached to one side for cleaning blackboards. If a student didn't duck in time, they were sure to get hurt and most likely bleed.) To ensure good behavior in the classroom, children were either caned or shamed. For some adults, the emotional scars of such corporal punishment endure to this day.

For those who can't identify with the above example, the principle of forceful, dictatorial leadership is perhaps universally understood through the example of Hitler. His dictatorship serves as a clear illustration of absolute control and the silencing of opposition. Similarly, Roman authorities, including Herod in the New Testament period, were known for their ruthless methods of enforcing "law and order." It was this context of ruthless power that Jesus directly addressed when he said, "You know that the rulers of the Gentiles lord it over them, and their high officials exercise authority over them. Not so with you" (Matt. 20:25–26).

Unfortunately, many despotic leaders dictate, pass orders, or make demands to supposedly obtain favorable results. However, Christ drew people with love and kindness instead of lording it over them. He delivered and saved us, not only to free us from the clutches of sickness, sin, and the Devil but also to allow us to rebuild our lives by living in relationship with him. His example prompts us to consider this approach in disciple-making: "This is how we know what love is: Jesus Christ laid down his life for us. And we ought to lay down our lives for our brothers and sisters" (1 John 3:16).

Defining Draw

"Draw" implies attraction or gentle persuasion. Though the word "draw" is not frequently used in the Scriptures, we see an overarching theme of God gently persuading and wooing his people with love.

Martin Luther, the seminal figure of the sixteenth-century Protestant Reformation, once commented on the word "draw" in John 6:44 ("No one can come to me unless the Father who sent me draws them, and I will raise them up at the last day"). Luther stated that the Father's drawing is "not like that of the executioner, who draws the thief up the ladder to the gallows; but it is a gracious allurement, such as that of the man whom everybody loves, and to whom everybody willingly goes."[1]

The following points highlight how Christ drew people to himself in his earthly ministry.

---

[1]   "John 6 Vincent's Word Studies," BibleHub, accessed August 23, 2022, https://biblehub. com/commentaries/vws/john/6.htm.

Jesus Performed Signs and Wonders

Though large numbers of people were drawn to Christ because of his miracles, he did not perform these miracles on demand; in fact, he was wary of performing miracles among crowds who were indifferent or unbelieving. Christ performed some signs and wonders—such as the calming of the sea, walking on water, the transfiguration, and the dying of the fig tree—to the Twelve, to perhaps reinforce his lordship to the faithful few. The miraculous catch of fish prompted Peter to fall to his knees as he recognized his sinfulness. He then chose to leave all and follow Christ, along with the other disciples (Luke 5:1–11).

Jesus Delivered and Healed

Christ drew people to himself not only through gentle teaching and acts of compassion but also through the way he authoritatively exercised his power over the demonic world. His presence or authoritative word was more than sufficient to expel demonic forces.

We read in Mark 3:14, "He appointed twelve that they might be with him and that he might send them out to preach," and Mark 3:15 continues, "and to have *authority* to *drive* out demons" (emphasis mine). The words "authority" and "drive" are quite the opposite of draw. While "draw" suggests a gentle invitation, "authority" and "drive" imply the use of forceful command to cast out demons. This is not an exercise of physical violence but a demonstration of God's authority, the same authority bestowed on followers of Christ. When Christ remarks to the Seventy-Two about Satan, he uses the same commanding language: "I saw Satan *fall like lightning* from heaven. I have *given you authority* to *trample* on snakes and scorpions and *to overcome all* the power of the enemy; nothing will harm you" (Luke 10:18–19, emphasis mine).

The impact of this authoritative power was evident in the lives of those who followed Jesus. The women who supported Christ's mission were known as those who had been cured of evil spirits and diseases (Luke 8:2–3). Mary Magdalene, known for her devotion to Christ and the first one to see him risen, had been delivered from seven demons. These demonstrations of Christ's power over darkness served as a compelling draw, offering hope and freedom to those oppressed and pointing them toward the source of such authority—God.

God continues to demonstrate his power and love when healing people today, though he sometimes chooses not to, for reasons beyond our comprehension. He sent his disciples with the command to heal and deliver people from demonic forces (Luke 9:1), with the hope that those healed would be drawn to him and respond favorably to the message of the kingdom.

Jesus Modeled Sacrifice and Service

Although Jesus' supernatural demonstrations were certainly appealing, acts of humble service—such as washing the disciples' feet—were significant in drawing others to him. After he rose from the dead, Jesus could have dazzled his disciples into submission or reprimanded them for desertion. Instead, he humbly served them by preparing breakfast on the beach (John 21:10–14).

God's love for the world and his people can be seen throughout Scripture, but the ultimate act of love was shown through his son, Jesus Christ, who came to earth as a man. "Nothing disarms a person like love…. It was Christ loving people, His service to them, His ministry to them … that drew people to him."[2] Christ demonstrated love by becoming a servant in human likeness (Phil. 2:6–7). He offered hope and forgiveness and befriended outcasts. Moved with compassion, he loved them unconditionally by stopping to heal, including ungrateful lepers (Luke 17:11–19).

The word "sanctify" in Jesus' high priestly prayer clearly reveals how he set himself apart for God to serve others. "As you sent me into the world, I have sent them into the world. For them I sanctify myself,

---

[2]   Robert E. Coleman, Bobby Harrington, and Josh Patrick, *Revisiting the Master Plan of Evangelism* (USA: Exponential Resources, 2014), 15, https://my.exponential.org/ebooks/revisitingmasterplan/.

that they too may be truly sanctified" (John 17:18–19). The context reveals that his sanctification was not because he lacked power or needed cleansing. It reveals his commitment and dedication to fulfill his God-given task of giving his life away to others.[3]

Jesus Partnered with the Father and the Spirit

Before he drew people to himself, Jesus was deeply rooted and grounded in God the Father and served in the power of the Holy Spirit. Christ did not draw people to himself in his own power or strength. He reflected the Father's loving heart, a theme that begins in Genesis and grows to a crescendo during Christ's life. Jesus acted in partnership with the Father, and his yearning to love all humankind was based on God's love. John 15:9 states, "As the Father has loved me, so have I loved you. Now remain in my love."

At the start of his ministry, we read that the Spirit led Christ into the wilderness where he was tempted (Luke 4:1). Christ then launched his public ministry by confidently stating to the startled audience that he was the fulfillment of Isaiah 61: "The Spirit of the Sovereign Lord is on me, because he has anointed me to proclaim good news to the poor" (Luke 4:18). His ministry was always in the power of the Holy Spirit.

Jesus Engaged with Receptive People

Jesus did not isolate himself with a secluded community like that of the Essenes,[4] neither did he mobilize violent groups such as the zealots of his day to claim his sovereignty over Israel or the world.[5] He also did not aim to garner a huge following of fans. Instead, he drew

---

[3]   Coleman, Harrington, and Patrick, *Revisiting the Master Plan of Evangelism*, 34–35.

[4]   Encyclopedia.com, s.v. "Essenes," accessed March 11, 2025, https://www.encyclopedia.com/philosophy-and-religion/judaism/judaism/essenes.

[5]   Joel B. Green, Scot McKnight, and I. Howard Marshall, eds., *Dictionary of Jesus and the Gospels: A Compendium of Contemporary Biblical Scholarship* (Leicester: Inter Varsity Press, 1992), 714.

a small community of disciples to share life with him (Matt. 11:27) and together serve those who were lost. Christ frequently used people's homes for rest and fellowship, such as those of Lazarus and Peter. Experiencing Christ's power and sacrificial service within a community of like-minded disciples provided a sense of belonging. Except for personal quiet times with God the Father, Jesus spent almost all his waking hours with his disciples.

Jesus, along with his disciples, sacrificially and compassionately ministered to crowds, but he did not entrust himself to the crowds (Matt. 14:13–15; John 2:23–25). Though he demonstrated his supernatural power among crowds to meet various temporal needs, such as providing food or healing the sick, he prioritized giving himself to the few who had left all to follow him. To them he offered peace (John 16:33), joy (John 15:11), glory (John 17:22–24), the Holy Spirit as a comforter (John 14:16–17), and the keys to the kingdom (Matt. 16:19).

Jesus Renewed Broken Lives

Christ's offer of forgiveness and his identification with outcasts and those condemned drew many people to him. Zacchaeus repented when Christ took the first step of drawing near to him (Luke 19:1–10). After being moved by Christ's revelation, the Samaritan woman mobilized her whole village to hear him for themselves. They then testified that he was indeed the Savior of the world (John 4:1–42). When the religious crowd brought a woman caught in adultery, Jesus shielded her from shame and death by offering grace and dignity (John 8:1–11).

Above all, Christ's life on the earth was geared toward the cross, where he gave his life to provide salvation and redemption to everyone. While the gift of salvation and eternal life continues to be an offer to all (Matt. 20:28), God gives humans the right to choose (John 3:16–17). Christ's grace is potent enough to raise wretches and those in bondage to serve along with him, not as his subjects or slaves but as friends who reign with him (John 15:14–15; Eph. 2:3–6).

Christ's approach to discipleship was characterized by an irresistible magnetism rooted in God's love for all people. His sacrificial love—demonstrated most powerfully on the cross, where he forgave his executioners—drew people to him. This love, combined with the evident answers to prayer, created a compelling attraction. Although speaking truth and giving dedicated time are necessary components of disciple-making, they are ineffective without this foundation of love and belonging. It was this connection to Jesus, not outward displays, that identified Christ's followers: "When they saw the courage of Peter and John and realized that they were unschooled, ordinary men, they were astonished and they took note that these men had been with Jesus" (Acts 4:13).

Try It Out

Below are a few practices to help you reflect Christ's way of drawing others to God.

- **Cultivate a leadership style marked by grace and compassion in your family and beyond:** As a spouse, parent, and leader, consciously lean toward understanding and kindness rather than strict authority. Consider how offering grace might foster deeper connection and a more lasting spiritual influence than demanding compliance. (As a husband, parent, and leader, I wish I had been more gracious and compassionate rather than being authoritarian and often demanding. Though my methods may have got "results," in hindsight, I realize that offering kindness would've had a more lasting, kingdom impact.)

- **Explore and embrace the reality of spiritual authority as part of Christ's commission:** Actively consider the significance of the authority Jesus gave his followers, as highlighted in Mark 3:15, "to have authority to drive out demons." Don't overlook this aspect as a means of demonstrating Jesus' power and drawing others to him. Begin by praying for discernment regarding spiritual oppression in your context and for opportunities to exercise this authority in alignment with the Spirit's leading. Read the Gospels and follow Christ's example. (We need Christ's discernment to know when to exercise authority over that which is demonic and when to be loving among those who are like sheep without a shepherd. If Christ spent many of his waking hours in prayer, entrusting himself to God the Father and his Spirit, it will do us well to invest time with God. By immersing ourselves in God's Word and meditating on Christ, we gain the discernment necessary to serve effectively as his disciple-makers. I confess I used to be skeptical of anything supernatural; I valued preaching but failed to take note of the second part of Christ's command mentioned in Mark 3:15: "to have authority to drive out demons." I cannot discount the second half of Christ's mandate—it is one way we can show the authority of Jesus and draw others toward him.)

- **Reflect on your relationships and identify 2–3 people with whom you feel a genuine connection and who seem open to spiritual conversations:** These are the people you will invest in most deeply.

- **Create intentional space:** Schedule regular time to connect with these individuals. This could be done via a weekly call, a formal meeting at a home or a restaurant, or during your lunch break.

- **Focus on genuine sharing:** Be authentic and vulnerable in your interactions. Share your own struggles, questions, and experiences with faith. This builds trust and creates a safe space for them to share.

Meditate and Discuss

Reflect on what the following verses reveal about how the Lord draws people to himself.

- "In your unfailing love you will lead the people you have redeemed. In your strength you will guide them to your holy dwelling" (Exod. 15:13).

- "The LORD is compassionate and gracious, slow to anger, abounding in love. He will not always accuse, nor will he harbor his anger forever" (Ps. 103:8–9).

- "He tends his flock like a shepherd: He gathers the lambs in his arms and carries them close to his heart; he gently leads those that have young" (Isa. 40:11).

- "The LORD appeared to us in the past, saying: 'I have loved you with an everlasting love; I have drawn you with unfailing kindness'" (Jer. 31:3).

- "When Israel was a child, I loved him, and out of Egypt I called my son.... I led them with cords of human kindness, with ties of love. To them I was like one who lifts a little child to the cheek, and I bent down to feed them" (Hos. 11:1, 4).

- "No one can come to me unless the Father who sent me draws them, and I will raise them up at the last day" (John 6:44).

- "'And I, when I am lifted up from the earth, will draw all people to myself.' He said this to show the kind of death he was going to die" (John 12:32–33).

- "But because of his great love for us, God, who is rich in mercy, made us alive with Christ even when we were dead in transgressions—it is by grace you have been saved" (Eph. 2:4–5).

- "See what great love the Father has lavished on us, that we should be called children of God! And that is what we are!" (1 John 3:1).

? *Any Questions?*

 *Any Ideas?*

 *Anything That Touches Your Heart?*

INFLUENCE

I used to think being busy with ever-increasing crowds was influence, but I've come to realize that lasting, impactful influence involves being focused on the few whom God has chosen and entrusted to me.

MILLIONS OF VOLUNTARY groups attribute their success to the principles he laid out in his writings, which have since been adopted and promoted in many diverse and creative forms. His influence continues to spread worldwide because of how he inspired and mobilized people toward personal transformation. What's most striking is his example: When he turned ninety in 2021, colleagues at Cooper Institute acknowledged that, "At age 90 and having logged more than 80,000 miles exercising daily, primarily running and now walking and cycling, Dr. Cooper sets the example for maintaining a healthy lifestyle by exercising."[1] Dr. Kenneth Cooper both coined the term "aerobics" and is widely regarded as the father of the discipline.

---

[1] The Cooper Institute, "Legendary 'Father of Aerobics' Dr. Kenneth H. Cooper Turned 90," Kenneth H. Cooper Institute, May 12, 2021, https://www.cooperinstitute. org/2021/05/12/legendary-father-of-aerobics-dr-kenneth-h-cooper-turned-90.

By their very nature, aerobics groups are decentralized, voluntary, autonomous gatherings of individuals who choose to exercise regularly, based on their fitness levels and desired outcomes. Though there are certified trainers, Dr. Cooper did not design aerobics as a hierarchical empire or a brand that profited him alone. Instead, he influenced others by his example and by sharing his ideology through the media. This eventually led to a movement of healthier people across the world. A quick perusal of aerobics videos on YouTube reveals how it has morphed into various styles and intensities.

In contrast to Dr. Cooper's approach, many institutions or enterprises have monopolized and monetized their ideology or discovery to gain control. Their "discovery" is not freely available or accessible. It comes at a high cost, benefiting only the creators. Not only was Dr. Cooper's example inspiring but his research on aerobics has also prompted people from all walks of life to emulate his lifestyle. Thousands have championed his ideas by becoming trainers or coaches. The profits and the benefits of applying aerobics are shared by all.

While Cooper's influence changed the physical fitness of many across the globe, Christ's influence in the realm of spirituality is incomparable. Jesus influenced his followers through love, which he exemplified throughout his life, culminating on the cross. He invested his time and trained a team of unschooled men from the shores of Galilee to serve as his ambassadors for peace. Despite tremendous hardship, they courageously crossed borders and influenced many others to form voluntary teams of Jesus-followers. Christ's offer of eternal life, hope, and peace is the same today and is available as a free gift to all. His influence continues to grow, as Samuel M. Lockridge highlights in *The Incomparable Christ*:

> More than nineteen hundred years ago, there was a Man born contrary to the laws of life. This Man lived in poverty and was reared in obscurity. He did not travel extensively. Only once did He cross the boundary of the country in which He lived; that was during His exile in childhood.

He possessed neither wealth nor influence. His relatives were inconspicuous and had neither training nor formal education.

In infancy He startled a king; in childhood He puzzled doctors; in manhood He ruled the course of nature, walked upon the waves as pavement, and hushed the sea to sleep.

He healed the multitudes without medicine and made no charge for His service.

He never wrote a book, and yet perhaps all the libraries of the world could not hold the books that have been written about Him.

He never wrote a song, and yet He has furnished the theme for more songs than all the songwriters combined.

He never founded a college, but all the schools put together cannot boast of having as many students.

He never marshaled an army, nor drafted a soldier, nor fired a gun; and yet no leader ever had more volunteers who have, under His orders, made more rebels stack arms and surrender without a shot fired.

He never practiced psychiatry, and yet He has healed more broken hearts than all the doctors far and near.

Once each week multitudes congregate at worshiping assemblies to pay homage and respect to Him.

The names of the past, proud statesmen of Greece and Rome have come and gone. The names of the past scientists, philosophers, and theologians have come and gone. But the name of this Man multiplies more and more. Though time has spread nineteen hundred years between the people of this generation and the mockers at His crucifixion, He still lives. His enemies could not destroy Him, and the grave could not hold Him.

He stands forth upon the highest pinnacle of heavenly glory, proclaimed of God, acknowledged by angels, adored by saints, and feared by devils, as the risen, personal Christ, our Lord and Savior.[2]

---

[2]   GIGM, "The Incomparable Christ," Growing in Grace Ministries, March 15, 2009, https://gigm.org/news/the-incomparable-christ/.

Defining Influence

There are positive and negative connotations to the word "influence." Negative examples include DUI (driving under the influence of alcohol or drugs), or the way 1 Corinthians 12:2 uses the word: "You know that when you were pagans, somehow or other you were influenced and led astray to mute idols."

However, more positively, "influence" implies gentle persuasion to bring about wholesome transformation. Nelson Mandela's influence, for example, brought lasting change. Richard Stengel, the author of *Mandela's Way*, records Mandela's words about leadership and influence.

> "You know, when you want to get the cattle to move in a certain direction, you stand at the back with a stick, and then you get a few of the cleverer cattle to go to the front and move in the direction that you want them to go. The rest of the cattle follow the few more energetic cattle in the front, but you are really guiding them from the back." He paused, "That is how a leader should do his work."[3]

The following points highlight how Christ's world-changing influence stemmed from investing deeply in his chosen disciples, whom he empowered, inspired, and guided by his example.

Jesus Focused on the Few

The appointment of the twelve disciples in Mark 3:14 ("He *appointed* twelve that they might be with him" [emphasis mine]) demonstrates the importance of personal connection in the way Jesus chose to influence others. This time of intimacy with Christ, however, was preparatory, as the verse continues, "and that he might send them out."

---

[3]   Ronald Wilde and Phillip Messina, "Leadership and Influence," ICMA, May 3, 2019, https://icma.org/articles/pm-magazine/leadership-and-influence.

The fact that he appointed a team of common folk *before* his public ministry shows us his reliance on people as the primary method.

This approach had little immediate impact on the religious or political world of his day, but when viewed in hindsight and from an eternal perspective, these men were being prepared to take the gospel to the ends of the earth, which continues to influence many today. As Robert Coleman notes in *The Master Plan of Evangelism*, "His concern was not with programs to reach the multitudes, but with men whom the multitudes would follow."[4]

Unlike rabbinic circles, in which disciples chose their master for a limited period, Christ chose a team who would serve him, in and through his Spirit, even after he left the earth.[5] Christ selected these disciples "from an existing network of relatives, business partners, neighbors and acquaintances."[6] They were mostly Galilean common folk with limited education and exposure (Acts 4:13). They did not have high credentials, positions of authority, or Levitical heritage from Jerusalem. The superficiality, hypocrisy, and cold legalism of religion around them did not deter their desire for the Messiah. It prompted some of them to join John the Baptist, who later pointed them to Christ (John 1:35–39). Others later joined the team as well. When we read the Gospels carefully, we can observe that Christ selected the Twelve within a span of one year, as Christ and the first few disciples ministered from place to place.[7]

Christ's intentional influence on a few disciples gave them ample opportunities to understand the source of his power. Observing Christ's character, lifestyle, and prayer times enabled the Twelve to grasp his commitment to spiritual disciplines and dependence on the Father. If Jesus had ministered and tried to influence others without a team, no one would have been made aware of these important values.

---

[4]   Coleman, *The Master Plan of Evangelism*, 21.

[5]   David Watson, *Discipleship* (London, UK: Hodder and Stoughton, 1981), 23.

[6]   Green, McKnight, and Marshall, *Dictionary of Jesus and the Gospels*, 177.

[7]   Coleman, *The Master Plan of Evangelism*, 21.

Among the Twelve, Christ focused his influence on a team of three: Peter, James, and John. The lists of the apostles given in the Gospels (see table 2.1) suggest that the Twelve were further subdivided into groups of four. In the passages from Matthew 10:2–4, Mark 3:16–19, and Luke 6:14–16, the first, fifth, and ninth names in each list are the same individuals. This may suggest that the "12 were organized into smaller units, each with a leader."[8] This again reinforces the value of close-knit teams that facilitate mutual edification. The idea of focusing on the few is evident in the way Jesus organized the Twelve.

Table 2.1: Organization of the Twelve Disciples Into Smaller Units

Matthew 10: 2–4	Mark 3:16–19	Luke 6:14–16
1. **Simon Peter**	1. **Simon Peter**	1. **Simon Peter**
2. Andrew	2. James	2. Andrew
3. James	3. John	3. James
4. John	4. Andrew	4. John
5. **Philip**	5. **Philip**	5. **Philip**
6. Bartholomew	6. Bartholomew	6. Bartholomew
7. Thomas	7. Mathew	7. Mathew
8. Mathew	8. Thomas	8. Thomas
9. **James Alphaeus**	9. **James Alphaeus**	9. **James Alphaeus**
10. Thaddaeus	10. Thaddaeus	10. Simon Zealot
11. Simon	11. Simon	11. Judas
12. Judas Iscariot	12. Judas Iscariot	12. Judas Iscariot

Jesus' emphasis on the few does not discount his concern for the crowds. Moved by compassion, he went out of his way to minister to crowds, often without sufficient rest or food. He involved the Twelve directly in this ministry, allowing them to witness firsthand his deep concern for every aspect of people's lives—emotional, physical, and spiritual. This hands-on model served as a powerful example for the disciples' future ministry.

---

[8]   Green, McKnight, and Marshall, *Dictionary of Jesus and the Gospels*, 148.

Furthermore, Jesus extended his influence beyond the Twelve by appointing seventy-two others and sending them out in pairs "to every town and place where he was about to go" (Luke 10:1). This strategic deployment, with teams working simultaneously in different locations, demonstrates his commitment to reaching as many people as possible with his message. It also provided the Seventy-Two with invaluable practical experience, allowing them to participate in the work of the ministry and experience the thrill of its impact for themselves:

> At that time Jesus, full of joy through the Holy Spirit, said, "I praise you, Father, Lord of heaven and earth, because you have hidden these things from the wise and learned, and revealed them to little children. Yes, Father, for this is what you were pleased to do."
>
> LUKE 10:21

These experiences—bearing witness to Jesus' compassion for the crowds, participating in ministry alongside him, and receiving Christ's commissioning—profoundly shaped the disciples. The fact that they were chosen, called, and commissioned significantly impacted the apostles, evidenced by their frequent references to this truth in many of their Epistles.

> In Christ we speak before God with sincerity, as those sent from God.
>
> 2 CORINTHIANS 2:17

> Peter, an apostle of Jesus Christ, To God's elect.
>
> 1 PETER 1:1

> For we know, brothers and sisters loved by God, that he has chosen you.
>
> 1 THESSALONIANS 1:4

Christ's influence in choosing and commissioning individuals had a profound impact on their sense of purpose and motivation. As David

Watson notes in his book *Discipleship*, "It is only when we begin to see ourselves as chosen, called and commissioned by Christ that we shall have any real sense of our responsibility to 'present our bodies as a living sacrifice, holy and acceptable to God.'"[9]

Jesus Led by Example

Christ's incarnation and the way he associated with his disciples provided a living example that powerfully influenced them, demonstrating how to live a life of service empowered by God's Spirit. The disciples were aware of Christ's dependence on the Father, the Scriptures, and prayer. They observed how he would withdraw to invest time in prayer, prompting them to ask him to teach them to pray (Luke 11).[10] They saw how he authoritatively and courageously confronted corrupt religious leaders. He went out of his way to show compassion and heal the sick and did not refrain from associating with those ostracized from society. He valued women and welcomed children, rather than ignoring them. These aspects of his lifestyle significantly influenced his disciples.

In Luke 8:1–2, Jesus demonstrated how they were to serve: "After this, Jesus traveled about from one town and village to another, proclaiming the good news of the kingdom of God. The *Twelve were with him*, and also some women who had been cured of evil spirits and diseases" (emphasis mine). Notice that there is no mention here of Jesus authorizing them to serve or heal; they were to simply observe him and be with him. Jesus was modeling for them the way they would eventually need to serve. Later on, Jesus said, "My mother and brothers are those who hear God's Word and put it into practice" (Luke 8:21). Jesus was not in haste to send them out before they had been able to observe how he served. Only after having demonstrated how they were to serve when they went into a particular town, did he

---

9   Watson, *Discipleship*, 21, quoting Romans 12:1.

10 Coleman, Harrington, and Patrick, *Revisiting the Master Plan of Evangelism*, 24.

appoint the Twelve and the Seventy–Two to do likewise (Luke 9:1–2; Luke 10:1).

Jesus Looked for Those Who Obeyed

Many people today measure influence by the number of "likes" on social media. Christ, however, did not gauge his influence by the large numbers who professed to believe in him. John 2:23–24 says, "Many people saw the signs he was performing and believed in his name. But Jesus would not entrust himself to them, for he knew all people." The call to discipleship is not mere belief, for the word "follow" implies total obedience, as the following verses suggest:

> If you love me, keep my commands.
>
> JOHN 14:15

> And Jesus said to them, "Come ye after me, [follow] and I shall make you to become fishers of men."
>
> MARK 1:17 YLT

> And whoever does not carry their cross and follow me cannot be my disciple.
>
> LUKE 14:27

Obedience involves cleaving steadfastly, conforming wholly to Christ's example in living, and if need be, dying as well. In *The Cost of Discipleship*, Dietrich Bonhoeffer says that legitimate and admirable pursuits or concerns based on "reason and conscience, responsibility and piety ... and 'even the law and scriptural authority'" could become formidable forces that prevent obedience.[11]

Christ could have dispensed information to produce scholars rather than coaching inconsistent men to be transformed and serve as his ambassadors to the world. Their transformation took place as they

---

[11] Bonhoeffer, *The Cost of Discipleship*, 69–75.

followed him, and after the day of Pentecost, nothing could stop them. While the process of selection and modeling are primarily God's initiative, commitment involves our choice and willingness to obey.

The importance of obedience is encapsulated in the Great Commission: "teaching them *to obey* everything I have commanded you" (Matt. 28:20, emphasis mine). As Christians, we often place far too much emphasis on rituals at the expense of emphasizing a daily walk, in submission to his will. Even practices such as reciting creeds, kneeling at the altar, or going through the waters of baptism can become meaningless, taking precedence over the need for a daily obedient walk with Christ.[12]

The disciples of Jewish rabbis would submit themselves as slaves to their masters for a time, until they became masters themselves. However, Christ expected a lifetime of unconditional obedience, as he laid down his life for the world.[13] Jesus expected obedience when he called Peter and Levi to leave all and follow him (Matt. 4:18–20; Mark 2:13–14). The story of the rich young ruler also highlights the need for single-minded obedience (Matt. 19:16–26).

Influence is not measured by crowds or public acclaim. The enduring influence of Christ, which continues to astonish, proves this. His method was not mass mobilization but concentrating on influencing the chosen few who left all and followed him wholeheartedly. As disciple-makers, we should emulate this approach, focusing on the few people God has entrusted to us and leading by example through obedient, sacrificial service.

---

12   Coleman, Harrington, and Patrick, *Revisiting the Master Plan of Evangelism*, 22.

13   Watson, *Discipleship*, 25.

Try It Out

Below are a few practices to help you reflect Christ's way of influencing others to God.

- **Spend time alone with God and his people:** Disciple-making must begin with the pervasive influence of Jesus. We cannot underestimate the power of his presence to shape and transform lives. People must be deeply influenced by Jesus before they can effectively serve. This influence comes through spending time with him, observing his life, and learning from his teachings. Spiritual formation is a unique process for each individual and cannot be mechanized or programmed in a standardized format to mass produce disciples. Sending people out to serve for the sake of obtaining results can be detrimental if they haven't had the opportunity to experience Christ for themselves. For example, a friend from a Hindu background was trained as a church planter and appointed to serve as a trainer of trainers. There was rapid growth, as thousands of discipleship groups sprang up across several states in India. However, he and his immediate family (who were also from a Hindu background) seemed to overlook the need to receive the influence of Jesus through consistently participating in worship and enjoying fellowship with a community of other disciples. Sadly, they are now dealing with depression, burnout, and discouragement.

  Spending time in Christ's presence and in the presence of other followers of Christ is essential. God's influence, guidance, and wisdom often comes when we are meditating on his Word in solitude. Listening, watching, and learning from others who exemplify Christ is essential. We all need a balance of rest and service.

- **Choose a few who can emulate your example:** Prayerfully choose people who can journey with you in the context of your work or ministry. Going through a book or Scripture is certainly helpful. However, it's even more impactful when disciple-makers and disciples share their lives together. For example, as a disciple-maker, your response when others hurt or mistreat you is an opportunity to exemplify Christlikeness. Allegiance to God is best observed or tested when important decisions need to be made or when there is a crisis. Hence, it is crucial for those of us who are disciple-makers to know how to respond like Christ and influence disciples by our example. At times, we may need to courageously assert our authority like Christ did at the temple (Mark 3:1–6); at other times, we may need to withdraw and pray earnestly, so that God's will is accomplished (Matt. 26:36–39).

Meditate and Discuss

Reflect on what the following verses reveal about how the Lord influences.

- "Be perfect, therefore, as your heavenly Father is perfect" (Matt. 5:48).
- "He appointed twelve that they might be with him and that he might send them out to preach and to have authority to drive out demons" (Mark 3:14–15).
- "No one can serve two masters. Either you will hate the one and love the other, or you will be devoted to the one and despise the other. You cannot serve both God and money" (Luke 16:13).
- "My sheep listen to my voice; I know them, and they follow me" (John 10:27).
- "Now that I, your Lord and Teacher, have washed your feet, you also should wash one another's feet. I have set you an example that you should do as I have done for you" (John 13:14–15).
- "You did not choose me, but I chose you and appointed you so that you might go and bear fruit—fruit that will last—and

so that whatever you ask in my name the Father will give you" (John 15:16).

- "Therefore, I urge you, brothers, and sisters, in view of God's mercy, to offer your bodies as a living sacrifice, holy and pleasing to God—this is your true and proper worship" (Rom. 12:1).
- "But God chose the foolish things of the world to shame the wise; God chose the weak things of the world to shame the strong" (1 Cor. 1:27).
- "To this you were called, because Christ suffered for you, leaving you an example, that you should follow in his steps" (1 Pet. 2:21).

 *Any Questions?*

 *Any Ideas?*

 Anything That Touches Your Heart?

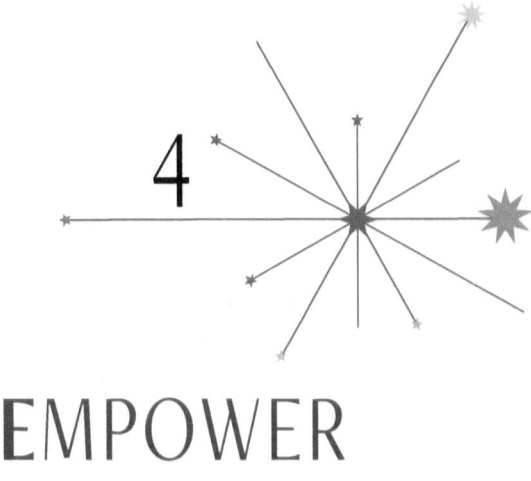

4

EMPOWER

I used to think that empowering involved striving to climb the ladder of success and then dispensing knowledge. But I've come to realize that empowering often involves showing restraint, stooping down, and doing whatever it takes to help others reach their full potential.

KANIYAPPAN IS AN eighty-five-year-old man featured in a thirty-minute documentary entitled *Adaiyaalam*, which means "identity" in Tamil. He was one of many Indian bonded laborers rescued from unscrupulous landowners. The landowners exploited Kaniyappan's debt to subject him to work under inhumane conditions at a woodcutting unit for several decades, with no hope of emancipation.[1] Kaniyappan wasn't allowed to leave the area, his food was rationed, and, to instill fear among the others, he was beaten in public view for minor offences. When he or any of the other laborers attempted to escape, the landowners tracked them down and forcibly brought them back. They were then subjected

---

[1] Karthikeyan M, "Adaiyaalam Documentary, Pain of Bonded labour, Iyan Karthikeyan, Irular Tribe," February, 9, 2021, YouTube, 30:29, https://www.youtube.com/watch?v=gugkerCPO5U&t=10s&ab_channel=KarthikeyanM; Roshne Balasubramanian, "Breaking Bondage," *The New Indian Express*, June 9, 2021, https://www.newindianexpress.com/cities/chennai/2021/jun/09/breaking-bondage-2313469.html.

to severe punishment and charged even more heavily on their already growing debt. Several bonded laborers were in servitude for generations.

Though the Indian government has outlawed bonded labor in the country since 1976, this practice continues, with an estimated 18.3 million people in some form of slavery.[2] One of the cofounders of the NGO who rescued Kaniyappan stated that it was primarily the victims' "lack of identity which further compounded the problem," while acknowledging the reality of "many structural and developmental reasons—from caste and class hierarchy to vulnerability and poverty that victimize[d] them."[3]

Similarly, although perhaps less overtly, an overview of church history reveals how a lack of spiritual identity and access to foundational truths has led to a form of spiritual subjugation, often unintentionally imposed by church leaders. For example, several centuries ago, the following two practices were commonplace:

- Church leaders, with the backing of state, outlawed ordinary believers from gathering in homes for worship and fellowship.
- Access to the Bible was restricted, and common people were not allowed to read it on their own.

Although these examples may not affect most of us today, followers of Christ can inadvertently neglect the exercise of their rights and privileges. This may stem from a lack of knowledge or faith, or from fears instilled by earthly authorities. Traditionalism or cultural customs can override the liberty found in Christ. Many sincere Christians continue to be ignorant and remain in spiritual bondage, held back by a lack of understanding of Scripture or failing to fully grasp the significance of their identity in Christ. I hope this attempt to briefly describe "the riches of his glorious inheritance" (Eph.1:18) will inspire us to

---

[2]   "India, Global Slavery Index," Global Slavery Index, accessed May 13, 2022, https://www. globalslaveryindex.org/2018/findings/country-studies/india/#footnote:12.

[3]   Balasubramanian, "Breaking Bondage."

delve deeper into God's Word to realize our full potential in Christ and what it means to be empowered by him.

Defining Empower

Two words in Greek—*exousia* and *endunamoó*—capture what "empower" means. *Exousia* implies "*conferred* power, *delegated empowerment*. It refers to the *authority* God gives to His saints—*authorizing them to act to the extent* they are *guided by faith*."[4] This use of the word "authority" is used in several passages. It refers to control, domain, dominion, and jurisdiction. Here are two significant passages where this word is used:

> Jesus called his twelve disciples to him and gave them authority to drive out impure spirits and to heal every disease and sickness.
>
> MATTHEW 10:1

> Then Jesus came to them and said, "All authority in heaven and on earth has been given to me. Therefore, go and make disciples of all nations."
>
> MATTHEW 28:18–19

Endunamoó means to fill with power, strengthen, or make strong. It comes from the root word *dunamis,* meaning power, might, strength, force, ability, efficacy, or energy. The words "dynamite" and "dynamo" stem from this word. It refers to supernatural, miraculous power. "En" refers to in, on, at, by, or with. Therefore, *endunamoó* emphasizes the need to make strong, to endue with strength, to strengthen, or to enable.[5] Below are two familiar verses that use this term:

---

4 "Strong's Greek: 1849. Ἐξουσία (Exousia)—Power to Act, Authority," accessed May 18, 2022, https://biblehub.com/greek/1849.htm, emphasis original.

5 "Strong's Greek: 1743. Ἐνδυναμόω (Endunamoó)—to Empower," accessed May 18, 2022, https://biblehub.com/greek/1743.htm.

I can do all this through him who gives me *strength*.

> PHILIPPIANS 4:13, emphasis mine

Finally, be strong in the Lord and in his mighty *power*.

> EPHESIANS 6:10, emphasis mine

To empower involves giving someone legal authority or having the freedom or confidence to do something.[6] It also denotes supernatural strength. Some of the synonyms for empower are authorize, enable, license, and commission.[7]

Wielding official or legal authority is powerful enough, but even greater is the honor of exercising Christ's supernatural strength and heavenly authority vested in us.

This chapter highlights how Christ empowered his disciples. He gave them his identity, even as he delegated to them the responsibility to reproduce many other disciples of Christ. We must note that Christ did not immediately empower his disciples. He revealed his plan progressively as they followed him and personally experienced the way he demonstrated his love and compassion to everyone. He did not overwhelm the Twelve by immediately giving them the responsibility of going into all the world, although that was his intended plan. They were endued with power on the day of Pentecost (Acts 2) after a time of waiting (Luke 24:49).

In our disciple-making, if sufficient time hasn't been given to drawing and influencing (as explored in chapters two and three), a hasty attempt at empowering individuals can lead to negative

---

[6] *Cambridge Dictionary*, s.v. "legal," accessed April 9, 2025, https://dictionary.cambridge. org/dictionary/english/legal; *Cambridge Dictionary*, s.v. "freedom," accessed April 9, 2025, https://dictionary.cambridge.org/dictionary/english/freedom; *Cambridge Dictionary*, s.v. "confidence," accessed April 9, 2025, https://dictionary.cambridge.org/dictionary/english/confidence.

[7] *Collins Dictionary*, s.v. "empower," accessed May 18, 2022, https://www.collinsdictionary. com/dictionary/english/empower.

outcomes, such as failure, frustration, and erosion of trust. Individuals need sufficient time to be drawn to Jesus, influenced by him, and then to gradually be endued with power and responsibility as they journey in obedience.

The following points highlight how Jesus empowered his disciples during his earthly ministry.

Jesus Gave His Disciples a Newfound Identity in Him

The start of this chapter highlighted that one of the primary reasons for the enslavement of lower-caste individuals is their "lack of identity." When Christ appointed the Twelve (Mark 3:14), he gave them an identity based on himself. He empowered them by authorizing them to do tasks he himself had done. They were not given tasks to merely set the stage for Jesus the preacher and the miracle worker. They, in fact, represented him: "Anyone who welcomes you welcomes me, and anyone who welcomes me welcomes the one who sent me" (Matt. 10:40).

The empowering nature of a newfound identity in Christ pervades the Gospels and the Epistles. In John's Gospel, we read that Christ called his disciples his friends and indicates how he empowered them: "I no longer call you servants, because a servant does not know his master's business. Instead, I have called you friends, for everything that I learned from my Father I have made known to you" (John 15:15).

In Ephesians, Paul emphasizes several truths about the identity of Christ's followers. We are adopted sons and daughters (Eph. 1:5), fellow citizens (Eph. 2:19), members of his household, heirs, members of one body, and sharers together (Eph. 3:6).

We are not to consider ourselves as slaves designated to serve or stand at the threshold of a house to receive "baksheesh" (tips, leftovers). We are adopted sons and daughters, heirs, and friends entitled to feast at the Father's table.

Jesus Assigned Responsibilities

Depending on the need, Christ empowered his disciples by assigning them specific responsibilities at various times, such as arranging accommodation, organizing crowds, preparing a meal, distributing food, collecting leftovers, and handling other logistical tasks. However, he also gave them responsibilities that many would consider priestly in nature, such as baptizing believers while he engaged in preaching (John 4:1–2). Commenting on this, Robert Coleman shares in *Revisiting the Masterplan of Evangelism*,

> Remember, Jesus' disciples weren't really certified above others. They were just believers who went out. I see no reason why anyone who is faithful to the Lord shouldn't have the privilege of administering the baptism and even the sacrament. I belong to the Jesus model, where anyone who is a believer is also a minister, and as a minister of God, you are a priest of God. For that reason, you can administer the holy sacraments.[8]

In Luke 9—after Christ sent out the Twelve to preach, drive out demons, and heal the sick—Herod was afraid when he heard about the healings because he thought John the Baptist had risen from the dead. Christ later sent out the Seventy-Two to do the same. Christ's authority at work in and through the apostles would have certainly recalibrated their view of Christ and his kingdom, even more so as their courage and confidence soared. He empowered them by appointing them as apostles to carry out significant tasks.

Jesus Expected Results

Jesus' expectation that his disciples would reproduce disciples is evident right from the start of the apostles' appointment. "'Come,

---

8   Coleman, Harrington, and Patrick, *Revisiting the Master Plan of Evangelism*, 27.

follow me,' Jesus said, 'and *I will send you out to fish for people*'" (Matt. 4:19, emphasis mine).

In Mark 3:14–15, note the phrase "and that," which points to the motive or purpose of their appointment as apostles: "He appointed twelve that they might be with him and that he might send them out to preach and to have authority to drive out demons."

The need to "be with him" preceded the dual purpose of declaring God's Word to people and exercising authority over the demonic world. Being with Jesus involved observing and learning the way he modeled ministry and how he served harassed and helpless crowds (Matt. 9:36). He periodically encouraged the disciples to come away from the crowds, but it was never a permanent arrangement. This period of "being with" Jesus was crucial in empowering and equipping the disciples for the assignments that followed, such as when the Twelve and Seventy-Two were sent out (Luke 9–10)—experiences that served as a foretaste of Jesus' ultimate sending through the Great Commission (Matt. 28:19–20).

Christ affirmed and celebrated the apostles' successful endeavors when he had sent them out to preach, heal, and deliver (Luke 10:21).

By acknowledging Peter's confession of his divine identity (Matt. 16:16) and entrusting the "keys of the kingdom" (symbolizing power and authority) to the apostles and the church (Matt. 16:19), Jesus empowered them to actively participate in establishing and expanding his reign on earth. This reveals "the significance of human initiative in bringing it to pass."[9] Christ stated,

> And I tell you that you are Peter, and on this rock I will build my church, and the gates of Hades will not overcome it. I will give you the keys of the kingdom of heaven; whatever you bind on earth will be bound in heaven, and whatever you loose on earth will be loosed in heaven.
>
> MATTHEW 16:18–19

---

9   Coleman, *The Master Plan of Evangelism*, 101.

Christ trained the Twelve as apprentices by providing various opportunities, empowering them through learning to become fishers of men. However, the significance of being fishers of men only dawned on them much later. It wasn't until the Holy Spirit came upon them that they began to apply Jesus' Great Commission (Matt. 28:19–20). In Acts 1:8, Christ gives his ascension commissioning to the disciples, "But you will receive power when the Holy Spirit comes on you; and you will be my witnesses in Jerusalem, and in all Judea and Samaria, and to the ends of the earth." This encapsulates the weight of responsibility, the scope, the sphere of influence, and the strategy Jesus was entrusting to them: to reproduce disciples and advance God's kingdom. This was only possible because he had not only empowered them in the preceding years through on-the-job training but also because they would receive the empowering of the Holy Spirit.

Jesus Examined Efforts

In a 1993 article entitled "From Sage on the Stage to Guide on the Side," educationalist Alison King emphasized the value of active learning. This is best accomplished when the teacher serves as a "guide on the side" rather than as a "sage on the stage." Despite ongoing debate among educators, King brought to the fore the value of this approach, where teachers play a facilitative role, and students are encouraged to discover the truth for themselves through discussion or participation. King highlighted the importance of coaching, including regular feedback and debrief sessions, to ensure that skills are well-learned.[10]

Though Jesus was undoubtedly admired for being the sage on the stage who spoke with authority, there are ample examples in the Gospels of Jesus empowering his disciples by serving as a guide on the side. He provided constant feedback to his disciples as they ministered alongside him. He corrected their judgmental attitudes when they questioned whether the blind man's fate was due to his sin or the

---

[10]   Alison King, "From Sage on the Stage to Guide on the Side," College Teaching, Vol. 41(1), 1993, 30–35.

sin of his parents (John 9). And in Luke 10, after they reported on their ministry experience, Jesus redirected their focus of celebration to their relationship with him rather than the victory over Satan.

Christ spent more time with his disciples during the last year and especially the last week of his life. He gave instructions, modeled servanthood, and instituted practices they would need to apply after he physically left this world. These God-ordained teaching moments empowered the disciples by further sharpening both their skills and their walk with God.

Jesus Equipped the Body to Serve

Christ empowers his followers for kingdom service by endowing us with gifts to equip others. These gifts, which can be classified as ministry gifts or spiritual gifts, are often discovered through exploration, experimentation, or even by unknowingly practicing them, without a conscious awareness that we possess them.

Australian missiologist Alan Hirsch's excellent book *The Forgotten Ways* elaborates on the ministry gifts of apostle, prophet, evangelist, shepherd, and teacher (APEST), based on Ephesians 4:1–16. Traditional church models often emphasize the shepherd/teacher roles, while the apostolic and prophetic gifts are either ignored or referred to as "offices" that have ceased to exist since the New Testament era. Alan Hirsch rightly points out how imperative it is for the health of the church to value all of the gifts.[11]

Romans 12:6–8 and 1 Corinthians 12:4–11 emphasize that the spiritual gifts listed are for the benefit of all. These gifts are best discovered through experimentation in the context of a close-knit and trusted team. Experimentation in this context enables leadership and growth, minimizing the risk of lasting negative repercussions that could arise from premature or misapplied gifts in a larger setting. A close-knit team allows individuals to receive feedback, encouraging

---

[11] Alan Hirsch, *The Forgotten Ways: Reactivating Apostolic Movements* (Grand Rapids, MI: Brazos Press, 2016), chapter eight.

them to either explore another gift or to make appropriate changes with loving guidance.

In conclusion, although God's grace and power are immeasurable, they have no practical impact in our lives if we do not embrace and act upon our identity in Christ. The apostles, empowered by the Holy Spirit after Pentecost, serve as a potent example. Their courage and determination to fulfill God's divine purpose by his power could not be contained. They served and boldly declared the gospel, with no fear of any earthly authority, persecution, or even the threat of death. This is the Spirit-empowered confidence available to all who believe, knowing that God is "able to do immeasurably more than all we ask or imagine, according to his power that is at work within us, to him be glory in the church and in Christ Jesus throughout all generations, for ever and ever! Amen" (Eph. 3:20–21).

Try It Out

Below are a few practices to help you reflect Christ's way of empowering others.

- **Pursue a deeper knowledge of your identity in Christ and discern your gifts:** Whether we are disciples or disciple-makers, we constantly need to not only understand but also live out our identity in Christ. This includes knowing how the Lord has empowered us to serve him. We can do this more effectively when we understand and identify the gifts God has bestowed on us. Gaining a clear understanding of what Scripture says about our identity and how he has gifted us will show us what we need to do in different seasons of our lives. The daily practice of reading and studying his Word should be the norm for any of us who profess to be followers of Christ. This practice will enable us to be fruitful.

- **Study the book of Ephesians:** Whether you are new in the faith or have been following Jesus for years, studying the book of Ephesians can bring valuable insights. It highlights the great extent to which Christ has empowered us and how he has raised us to serve with him, using the gifts he has bestowed on us. Take note of the need to serve *with* him, not merely serve him. The Lord desires to work with us, and we will be so much more fruitful when we serve in partnership with him. Intentionally take time with your close-knit group of fellow believers to explore and exercise various gifts that are mentioned in Scripture. Their feedback, encouragement, and suggestions, along with your own assessment, will enable you to identify the gifts God has given you.

- **Identify reliable people:** As a disciple-maker, you will need to exercise discernment to identify those who are trustworthy and reliable, so that you can focus your energies on the few God entrusts to you. There are many fans and excited people who profess to love and follow Christ, but there are only a few who will choose to go the distance to personally apply and relay the truths to others.

  Apart from seeking the Lord in prayer, a practical way to identify potential disciples is by assigning responsibilities, defining the expected outcomes, and evaluating their efforts and the results. This might start with practical responsibilities such as setting the furniture for a gathering or cleaning up after everyone has left. You might then move them on to other types of responsibilities, such as coordinating prayer times, leading worship, or facilitating Bible studies. Of course, this delegation should be done with humility, not in a domineering manner. For example, when assigning dishwashing, working alongside the person models and teaches the value of humble service.

Once reliable people are identified, it is important that you invest a good portion of your time to equip and empower them and later to launch them to serve on their own. (The chapter on mentoring has more practical insights on this theme.)

Meditate and Discuss

Reflect on what the following verses reveal about how the Lord empowers.

- "Jesus called his twelve disciples to him and gave them authority to drive out impure spirits and to heal every disease and sickness" (Matt. 10:1).
- "He said to them, 'Go into all the world and preach the gospel to all creation'" (Mark 16:15).
- "When the apostles returned, they reported to Jesus what they had done. Then he took them with him and they withdrew by themselves to a town called Bethsaida" (Luke 9:10).
- "You did not choose me, but I chose you and appointed you so that you might go and bear fruit—fruit that will last—and so that whatever you ask in my name the Father will give you" (John 15:16).
- "And God is able to bless you abundantly, so that in all things at all times, having all that you need, you will abound in every good work" (2 Cor. 9:8).
- "For we are God's handiwork, created in Christ Jesus to do good works, which God prepared in advance for us to do" (Eph. 2:10).
- "But you are a chosen people, a royal priesthood, a holy nation, God's special possession, that you may declare the praises of him who called you out of darkness into his wonderful light. Once you were not a people, but now you are the people of God; once you had not received mercy, but now you have received mercy" (1 Pet. 2:9–10).

 **Any Questions?**

 **Any Ideas?**

 **Anything That Touches Your Heart?**

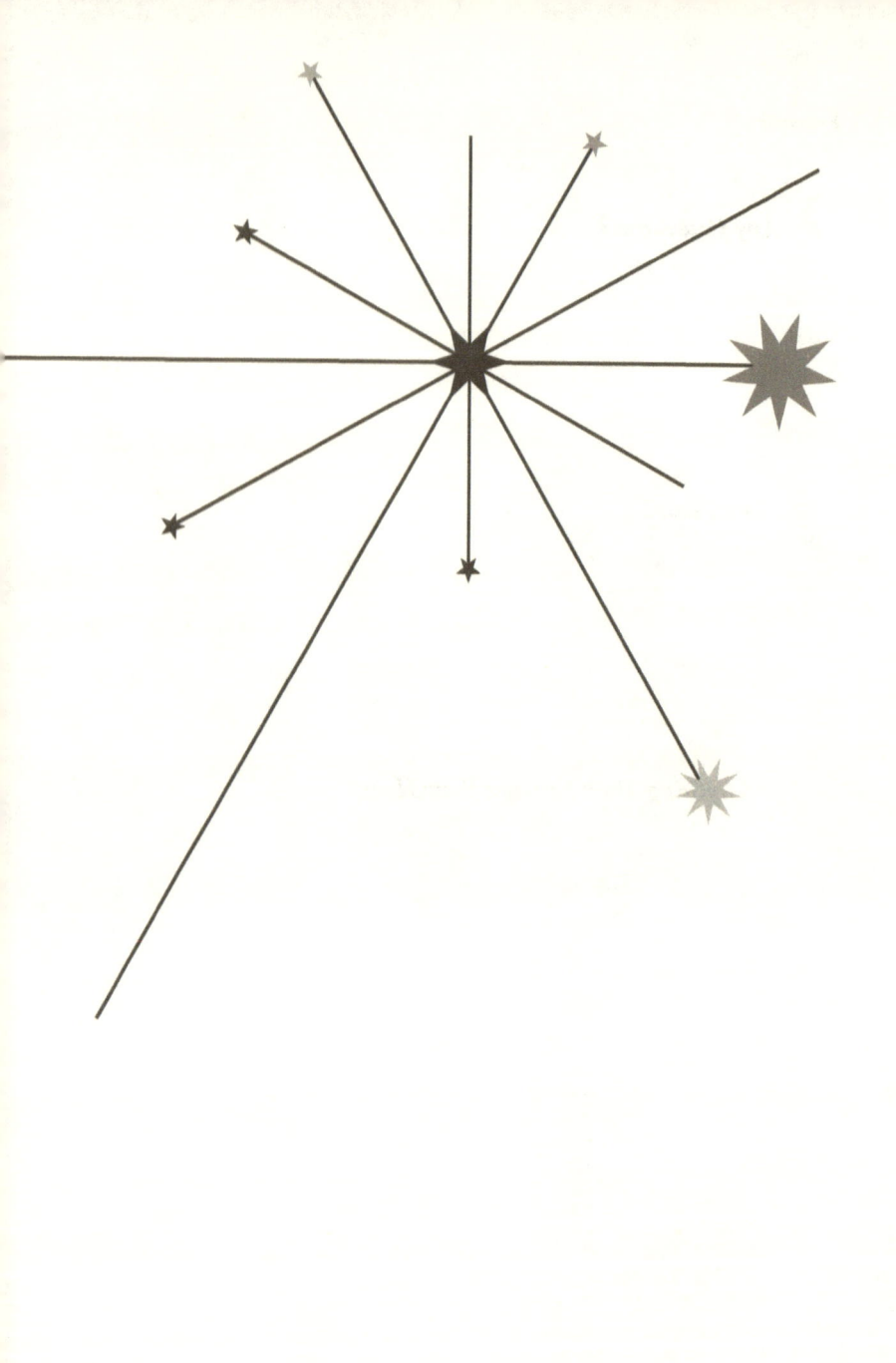

TEAMS

Our Responsibility as God's Church

*I used to think church was just about songs and sermons,
but I've come to realize it's about sacrifice and service, as
individuals and in Christ-centered teams.*

IN PART ONE, we explored the foundational principles of God's
initiative in forming the church through his love, encapsulated in the
acronym DIE: draw, influence, and empower. We explored how God,
through Christ's selfless sacrifice, draws people to himself, influences
them with his love, and empowers them to serve as his followers.

Now, in part two, we shift our focus to the practical outworking of
these principles in our daily lives as members of his church, in response
to God's love and the Spirit's work in our lives. This section guides us
through actionable steps and responsibilities that we, as followers of
Christ, must undertake to live out our faith effectively. In chapter five,
we first learn from the early church and early Methodism to explore
how they embodied the functions of TEAMS: teaching, evangelism,
adoration, mentoring, and sharing—all of which are essential for the
spiritual health and growth of the church and its members. We also
address the need to move away from traditional, institutional views
toward a more dynamic, relational, and mission-focused approach.

By redefining how we understand and practice being the church, we can better reflect the true nature and mission of the church as a community of Christ's disciples.

Chapters six through ten explore each of these functions in more detail. The conclusion highlights some practical steps to help you live as God's agent of change.

Although the emphasis of the various functions of TEAMS primarily focuses on how they can be practiced within the context of small teams, I also intentionally highlight personal disciplines, because a team is only as strong as its weakest link. A team's maturity and fruitfulness are dependent on every member's participation as they use their gifts, based on the overflow of their personal commitment to God (Eph. 4:11–16).

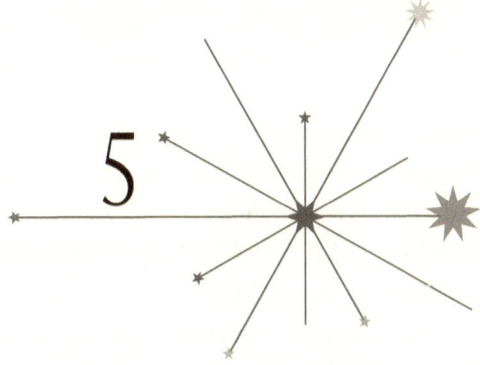

5

RETHINKING CHURCH

I used to be on edge while setting the stage for church on Sundays and failed to demonstrate that being church is a 24/7 responsibility to serve and bless others.

DURING THE NEW Testament period, the Greek word for "church" was *ekklésia*, which was a secular term referring to a group of people who were called out from the community and summoned by a herald.[1] It originally had no religious connotations; in fact, it had more to do with a political gathering at a specific location.

When the Hebrew Old Testament was translated into Greek, the secular Hebrew word *kahal*, meaning a "meeting of the people summoned together,"[2] was consistently translated into the Greek word *ekklésia*. This word is used about a hundred times in the Old Testament. It is often qualified by the phrase "of the Lord," implying that these gatherings were of God and for God. As Swiss priest Hans Küng notes, "God gathers together and the *ekklesia* therefore becomes

---

[1]   Joseph Thayer and James Strong, "Thayer's Greek: 1577. Ἐκκλησία (Ekklésia)—an Assembly, a (Religious) Congregation," accessed April 23, 2015, http://biblehub.com/thayers/1577.htm.

[2]   "BDB Hebrew: 6951. לְהָק (Qahal)—Assembly, Convocation, Congregation," accessed April 23, 2015, http://biblehub.com/bdb/6951.htm.

a community of God ... the congregation of those previously chosen by God, who gather round God as their center."[3] Since God chooses and gathers the community—the *ekklesia*—it is an abstract, invisible global body that only God knows. 2 Timothy 2:19 says, "The Lord knows those who are his."

The words "community" and "congregation" are intrinsically linked with "church," and the terms are often used interchangeably to describe a consistent local group rooted in Christ and in close fellowship with each other. Therefore, the church isn't a gathering of disconnected spectators who merely watch and hear great sermons or "enjoy" worship as individuals. Furthermore, the local church cannot be viewed as an independent or self-sufficient religious entity. It must embrace interdependence because the local body is also part of the global church.

In other words, the church is a community of lifelong apprentices centered on Christ, who learn by trial and error as they serve God and others. New Testament scholar Michael Wilkins writes, "Since all true Christians are disciples, the ministry of the church may be seen in its broadest sense as 'discipleship.'"[4] Therefore, discipleship should not be considered as an optional appendage or program of the church. Church and discipleship go together. Outward steps such as paying a subscription (which is prevalent in some denominations), signing a statement of faith, or becoming an official member of a church denomination or local church do not mean that an individual is a disciple. These steps may be helpful, but it is presumptuous to think that they identify a person as Christ's disciple.

Spaces for the People of God

Given the way the word "church" is used in the Old and New Testaments, we can conclude that congregating as a community

---

3   Hans Küng, *The Church* (Garden City, NY: Image Books, 1976), 118.

4   Michael Wilkins, *Following the Master: A Biblical Theology of Discipleship* (Grand Rapids, MI: Zondervan, 1992), 42.

is essential for the church. While physical gathering places were undoubtedly important for both the Israelites and the early church, helping to shape their communities, they were not permanent. The church, being a community of disciples, was never dependent on any specific location. God communicated with his people irrespective of the places where they gathered. (See the appendix for details.)

Through studying Scripture, we can observe that God communicated with his people, with or without human-made physical structures. Leading up to the establishment of the tabernacle (approximately three thousand years after the Genesis creation), God used various supernatural ways to communicate with his people. Later, the tabernacle and the temple—managed by priests—served as visible structures to connect with God. However, both were destroyed. During the Exile, synagogues served as a place for worship, learning, and fellowship.[5] In the Gospels, we read that Christ used the temple, synagogues, homes, and any other suitable areas to boldly proclaim his message. In Acts, we read that the apostles did the same. However, when persecution mounted in Jerusalem, people were forced to disperse and some even had to abandon their homes. These Jewish believers were forcibly ejected from their communities but continued to share the gospel wherever they went, and the church grew exponentially in multiple locations. This points to the foundational premise of this book: that teams of Christ-followers who are disciple-makers can indeed be the church as agents of change, *wherever* they are scattered.

Beyond Location: People of the Way as a Mobile Movement

Christ used any available space to proclaim the kingdom. The Gospels record Jesus proclaiming his message and performing miracles on the road, in fields, on mountains, and even in the midst of a raging sea. Despite Jesus also using various religious venues, *he did not*

---

5   "Synagogue, Definition, History, and Facts," Britannica, March 8, 2025, https://www. britannica.com/topic/synagogue.

commission his disciples to go into all the world and build temples, synagogues, or even houses. Instead, he expected his followers to leave all and follow him, including laying aside genuine family obligations (Luke 9:57–62).

Luke's emphasis in the book of Acts was not so much about *where* they met for worship and proclamation but on *how* the Holy Spirit broke through among various ethnic groups, as teams of Christ's disciples obeyed him wholeheartedly. When persecution broke out in Jerusalem, followers of the Way were people who practiced their faith in homes but were also part of the synagogues.

> Saul began to destroy the church. Going from *house to house,* he dragged off both men and women and put them in prison.
>
> ACTS 8:3, emphasis mine

> Saul was still breathing out murderous threats against the Lord's disciples. He went to the high priest and asked him for letters to the *synagogues* in Damascus, so that if he found any there who belonged to the Way, whether men or women, he might take them as prisoners to Jerusalem.
>
> ACTS 9:1–2, emphasis mine

Despite the outbreak of persecution, the scattered disciples multiplied even further. People of Samaria believed as they saw signs and wonders; later, the Ethiopian encountered Christ through Philip on the desert road (Acts 8). Acts 11 narrates how homeless refugees or exiles spread the gospel as they scattered due to persecution. Some even crossed cultural borders to testify among the Gentiles.

> Now those who had been scattered by the persecution that broke out when Stephen was killed traveled as far as Phoenicia, Cyprus and Antioch, spreading the word only among Jews. Some of them, however, men from Cyprus and Cyrene, went to Antioch and

began to speak to Greeks also, telling them the good news about the Lord Jesus. The Lord's hand was with them, and a great number of people believed and turned to the Lord.

ACTS 11:19–21

The early church consisted of people who had courageously stepped out in faith to follow Christ, even to the point of death. They boldly stood their ground and were willing to pay the highest price—laying down their lives—when Jewish religious authorities attacked them or when they refused to worship the Roman emperor. They were like scattered sheep but with a good Shepherd. Notice how Peter addresses the early Jewish Christ-followers.

Peter, an apostle of Jesus Christ, To *God's elect, exiles scattered* throughout the provinces of Pontus, Galatia, Cappadocia, Asia and Bithynia.

1 PETER 1:1, emphasis mine

For "you were like sheep going astray," but now you have *returned to the Shepherd and Overseer* of your souls.

1 PETER 2:25, emphasis mine

The people of the Way may have included those who worshipped in the temple, the synagogues, or homes; but one undeniable fact is that they were close-knit disciples who functioned as a family. They were Christ-centered *teams* who impacted people wherever they went. Whether scattered or exiled (Acts 11:19–20), they courageously took God at his Word; and, empowered by the Holy Spirit, announced the good news to all. Unlike today's perception and practice, church was a radical movement of Christ-centered disciples, mobilizing others to follow Jesus. Church was definitely not a static, "holy" place, where only talented individuals showcased their "gifts" on stage, to offer a great "service."

A Rationale for Teams to Function as the Church

The early church was thus made up of voluntary communities of Christ-followers who gathered in various venues, be it in the temple, the synagogues, homes, or any other location, primarily to edify one another. But almost all of these venues were short-lived meeting places, including people's homes. What thrived in the face of persecution or famine was the idea of fraternities—close-knit teams of Christ's disciples—who were forced underground or scattered as exiles and refugees. Can the scattered diaspora—who boldly proclaimed Christ wherever they went, while fleeing persecution—be considered any less a church, because they did not gather in a building?

Comparing the various venues of the early church mentioned above to our present-day structures, we can conclude that megachurch buildings can indeed continue to be great venues for Christ-followers to celebrate Jesus and hear the preaching of God's word. However, these venues are often only effective in larger cities due to the concentration of people and resources they require in order to thrive. Medium-sized church communities that gather in brick-and-mortar structures continue to serve in local regions in meaningful ways. The resurgence of home churches in the past few years has facilitated intimacy and fellowship. All these spaces—from the megachurch to the home—have been useful, but they cannot be viewed as permanent structures for discipleship to thrive. The use of these spaces—including people's homes—is becoming difficult or even dangerous, given current trends such as increasing building maintenance costs, rising hostility in some areas, war, persecution, or government interference to curtail the gospel. However, close-knit, Christ-centered teams that edify and hold one another accountable can thrive in any situation. They are needed now more than ever. Such teams need to be considered as the church. They cannot be viewed as a subset of a larger body that gathers on a Sunday. What are we implying when we term the large Sunday gatherings as "church," but then refer to the weekly neighborhood gatherings as "small groups"? Wouldn't things stir and perspectives change if we referred to the larger Sunday gathering as "the big group" and the smaller gatherings as "the church"?

The concept of teams or committed fraternities under Christ's lordship—which can gather anywhere under any circumstance, even in the face of opposition—needs to be validated. These teams can transform their spheres of influence with Christ's presence and glory.

In the book of Daniel, for example, Shadrach, Meshach, Abednego, and Daniel had no access to the temple, to synagogues, or even their family homes. Yet they tenaciously held onto their faith and took courageous steps of obedience, gaining the attention of the Babylonian king and his officials. In the book of Esther, the courage and faithfulness of two cousins, Esther and Mordecai, saved the people of Israel from annihilation. Although displaced and removed from venues of worship and fellowship, God changed their world as they held on to their convictions together and courageously took steps for the glory of God. The Lord used these teams to bring transformation, by his Spirit—even in the Old Testament.

In Acts 2, when the early believers responded to Peter's sermon, and after the Holy Spirit came upon them, they devoted themselves to various functions to mature in their faith. Their devotion was evidence of God's Spirit at work within them. When we observe the number of times the word "they" is either stated or implied in Acts 2:36–47, we can see that the people functioned as a team, instinctively and voluntarily taking steps to communally draw closer to God. *They* devoted themselves to the apostles' teaching, *they* were devoted to fellowship, *they* were devoted to the breaking of bread, *they* were devoted to prayer, *they* shared with one another, *they* met in homes. The descriptions in this passage do not give the impression that the apostles micromanaged every event. It does not appear that the leadership organized details of the home gatherings or had to persuade people to participate. Maybe it was part of the apostles' teaching, but from the way Luke describes these events, it appears that the people responded spontaneously. It was a voluntary initiative from the ground up rather than driven by a top-down approach. Acts 2:42 does not read that the apostles devoted themselves to preach Christ's teaching, or that they were devoted to lead and direct people to be engaged in prayer, fellowship, or the breaking of bread. There is no indication from this passage that the apostles were highly organized managers and motivators. We can be sure, however, that it was the Spirit who prompted the people to instinctively take on the responsibility of growing by themselves.

Christ's indwelling power enables teams of disciples to rapidly multiply and bring about significant transformation. Having a committed team of disciples and intentionally spurring one another on to serve with a sense of purpose is far more fruitful than merely gathering, even if this gathering is in a house. Am I referring to a ministry team? Yes, I sure am. Every team can function as church and prayerfully fulfill a task with a mission focus, based on its giftedness. A mission focus is essential for a group that is centered on Christ. Without this focus, members can become inward-looking. Many house churches have lost their effectiveness by being overly focused on themselves. For example, food, fellowship, and the comfort level between close-knit friends can desensitize a group from the realities beyond themselves. Balance in fulfilling various functions is necessary; there needs to be a commitment to evangelism, proclamation, and obedience of the Word, to fellowship in the breaking of bread, to prayer, and sharing (Acts 2:14–47).

The Early Church's Expression of TEAMS

Having highlighted how households in Jerusalem took steps to devote themselves to various functions to mature in their faith, I have arranged these functions as the acronym TEAMS (teaching, evangelism, adoration, mentoring, and sharing). TEAMS also underscores the truth that they are indeed the church. Below is a brief overview of the Jerusalem church's expression of TEAMS. (The subsequent chapters provide more insight into these functions.)

Teaching: This can be observed in the way the early believers devoted themselves to the apostles' teaching (Acts 2:42–46). Peter's sermon in Acts 2:14–41 also reveals his insight and commitment to the Scriptures. Furthermore, the gatherings in homes, as indicated in 1 Corinthians 14:26, had a culture of mutual teaching and learning, where believers actively edified one another through shared insights and experiences.

Evangelism: Acts 2 describes how Peter courageously declared the good news of Christ's salvation, and three thousand responded favorably. We also read that the Lord added to their number daily (Acts 2:14, 40–41, 47). In Acts 4, when the Sanhedrin commanded Peter and John not to speak in the name of Jesus, Peter and John boldly stated that they'd rather obey God than men (Acts 4:18–20). The spread of the gospel also significantly occurred through the compelling community life of smaller groups from the Jerusalem church, characterized by their unity and joyful interactions in homes, which drew others to their faith. For instance, the believers in Jerusalem regularly met in homes for fellowship and meals, displaying "glad and sincere hearts" (Acts 2:46) and "praising God" (Acts 2:47), creating a powerful witness within their local contexts. Furthermore, the positive favor they held with the wider population (Acts 2:47) suggests that their close-knit community and evident joy served as an attractive testimony. The consistent fellowship and shared life within these smaller groups emanating from the Jerusalem church played a vital role in the early growth of the Christian movement.

After the persecution in Jerusalem scattered the believers, "those who had been scattered preached the word wherever they went" (Acts 8:4), suggesting small teams or individuals from the Jerusalem church actively evangelizing in new locations through personal encounters and smaller gatherings outside the city.

Adoration: Adoration to Christ can be observed by the early church's devotion to prayer and praise when they gathered in homes (Acts 2:42, 46–47). For example, in Acts 4:31, the church gathered to pray after the authorities released Peter and John, resulting in the meeting place being shaken and the believers being filled with the Holy Spirit.

Mentoring: Mentoring was a key aspect of the Jerusalem church. This is evidenced by their commitment to the apostles' teaching (Acts 2:42), where the apostles served as primary mentors and laid out the theological foundation of their faith. The church's commitment to its mentors and the needs of the community is powerfully illustrated by its radical generosity in bringing the proceeds from the sale of properties and laying them at the apostles' feet. Mentoring also manifested in the community's reciprocal support and encouragement. For example, Barnabas (a respected member of the Jerusalem church) played a crucial role in vouching for the newly converted Paul (Acts 9:27) and later in co-leading and guiding him in ministry (Acts 11:25–26).

Sharing: This is quite evident in the way the early church gathered daily in homes, to share food, their lives, and their resources with one another (Acts 2:44–47; 4:32, 34–37).

Learning from Early Methodism

The importance of committed, Christ-centered teams that function as the body of Christ and bring about transformation in their communities was evident in the principles and practices of early Methodism. We have much to learn from early Methodism's powerful impact. In the early eighteenth century, John Wesley and his followers sparked a movement that would transform the spiritual landscape of England and beyond. This movement, known as Methodism, was characterized by its disciplined approach to discipleship and its emphasis on small, accountable groups. Wesley's innovative methods and organizational structure played a crucial role in the rapid growth and lasting impact of the early Methodist movement.

The significance of Methodism lies in its ability to mobilize ordinary people for extraordinary ministry. Wesley's approach was not limited to the educated or the elite; it empowered ordinary men and women to take on significant roles in the church and society. By organizing believers into classes, bands, and societies, Wesley created a system that fostered deep spiritual growth, mutual accountability, and active service.

Just as Wesley's methodical approach led to a revival that changed the course of history, we, too, can learn from these principles to ignite a movement of discipleship and service in our contexts.

The early Methodists demonstrated that the church is not merely a place or an event, but a dynamic community of believers devoted to following Christ and making disciples. They demonstrated that genuine spiritual growth happens in the context of close-knit, accountable relationships.

The early Methodists' commitment to teaching, evangelism, adoration, mentoring, and sharing (TEAMS) can be applied in our own lives and communities. In the following chapters, we will explore how these functions, when practiced consistently and intentionally, can lead to a vibrant and transformative church that fulfills its responsibility as the body of Christ.

The lessons from early Methodism can inspire us to reimagine what it means to be the church today, to be agents of change, and to bring the light of Christ to a world in need. By embracing these principles, we can spark teams for change and see the church flourish in ways we never dreamed of.

A Brief History of Early Methodism

John Wesley's follow-up strategy of organizing those who responded to his sermons into smaller groups proved to be a crucial factor in fueling the Methodist movement. By 1738, Wesley had established and supervised several types of these groups, which, for the sake of alignment with this book's themes, we'll refer to as "teams." This structure, known as the Methodist system, facilitated regular meetings in homes or simple preaching houses and included quarterly love feasts. By the turn of the century:

- One in every thirty Englishmen were Methodists.
- Methodism was a significant movement of ordinary people.
- In the late 1700s, they were known to be the most disciplined, cohesive, and distinct group of people in England.[6]

Methodist societies consisted of classes and bands. The prerequisite to joining a society was membership in a class or a band. These were the "primary point of belonging" or "intimate level of community."[7] The Methodist societies were the sum total of class and band members.

The Class Meeting: Wesley did not design the classes for instruction, as the name suggests; each member reported on their spiritual progress. In response, the others would offer counsel, advice, correction, and prayer as each one shared their concerns. After an hour or two, the group concluded the meeting with thanksgiving and prayer. The group channeled monetary offerings, however small, through the leaders to the society, who dispensed the funds to traveling preachers and the poor. These classes functioned like house churches, situated in the various neighborhoods.[8]

The Bands: This was an even more intimate group of six, without an overseer to ensure and facilitate mutual responsibility. While classes accommodated those who were not believers, bands consisted of those who had an assurance of salvation. Like the classes, everyone reported their individual spiritual progress to each other, but they also confessed their sins to one another. Every member asked probing accountability questions to help each member to recognize known

---

[6] Howard Snyder, *The Radical Wesley and Patterns of Church Renewal* (Downers Grove; IL: InterVarsity Press, 1980), 2, 54, 125.

[7] Snyder, *The Radical Wesley and Patterns of Church Renewal*, 54.

[8] Snyder, *The Radical Wesley and Patterns of Church Renewal*, 54–55.

sins and confess them within the group. They asked each other the following questions:

- What known sins have you committed since our last meeting?
- What temptations have you met with?
- How were you delivered?
- What have you thought, said, or done, of which you doubt whether it be sin or not?[9]

Given the rigor and level of transparency within the group, the number of bands was fewer. About 20 percent of those who were part of the Methodist system met in bands, whereas all the others were engaged in classes.[10]

Select Society: The select society were people who had shown progress in their walk with God and were considered to be spiritually mature (not to be confused with the Methodist societies, which comprised regular members of bands and classes). The members were expected to be honest with one another, and discussions were private. Confidential matters were not to be repeated, even amongst themselves. They were submissive to one another and shared their resources to achieve a sense of equality and commonality.[11]

Traveling Lay Preachers: Wesley supervised traveling lay preachers and expected them to embrace poverty, follow strict rules, and obey God. He taught them to withstand pressure, be it from people or difficult weather conditions. These itinerant lay preachers helped sustain the groups that spread throughout the land.[12]

This system of classes, bands, societies, and lay preachers, along with other offices and functions, helped foster discipleship and the development of leaders in natural on-the-job settings. One in ten (and

---

[9] Snyder, *The Radical Wesley and Patterns of Church Renewal*, 60.

[10] Snyder, *The Radical Wesley and Patterns of Church Renewal*, 62.

[11] Snyder, *The Radical Wesley and Patterns of Church Renewal*, 62.

[12] Snyder, *The Radical Wesley and Patterns of Church Renewal*, 63.

perhaps even as many as one in five) within the Methodist system held significant ministry and leadership responsibilities.[13] Those who served as leaders were not typically educated, wealthy, or those with spare time on their hands. They were laboring men and women, young and old, husbands and wives who were eager to serve with the abilities and gifts they possessed. These close-knit Christ-centered teams "became the incubator and training camp for Christ-like ministry."[14] Wesley's commitment to this system was so strong that he refused to preach in any place where he could not follow it up with societies and able leadership.[15] "He was out to make disciples—disciples who would renew the whole church."[16]

Wesley's View of the Church

Early in his ministry, Wesley paid much attention to the form and function of the church. Commenting on Acts 5:11, he wrote that the church was "a company of [people], called by the gospel, grafted into Christ by baptism, animated by love, united by all kinds of fellowship, and disciplined by the death of Ananias and Sapphira."[17]

In a sermon entitled *Of the Church*, Wesley stated that the church was, in its proper sense, "a congregation or body of people united together in the service of God…. Even two or three united in Christ's name, or a Christian family, may therefore be called a church."[18]

In theory, Wesley had no reservations about considering a group of people to be the church, even if they had insufficient preaching of the gospel or improper administration of the sacraments—unlike the Anglicans, who refused to consider such folk to be even part of the

---

[13]   Snyder, *The Radical Wesley and Patterns of Church Renewal*, 63.

[14]   Snyder, *The Radical Wesley and Patterns of Church Renewal*, 63.

[15]   Sydney G. Dimond, *The Psychology of the Methodist Revival*, 6th ed. (London, UK: Oxford University Press, 1926), 112.

[16]   Snyder, *The Radical Wesley and Patterns of Church Renewal*, 64.

[17]   John Wesley, *Explanatory Notes upon the New Testament* (London: Epworth, 1958), 411.

[18]   Thomas Jackson, ed., *The Works of John Wesley* (London, UK: John Mason, 1829), VI, 371.

universal church.[19] Against the prevailing norm, Wesley was courageous to take the gospel to the poor and out onto the streets. But even
bolder was his practice of appointing common people to serve with
him as coworkers and leaders. His systematic approach to discipleship
through these teams—classes, bands, and select societies—was a key
factor in fueling revival, as scholars have widely noted.

Although Wesley's theories were biblical, in practice, his
allegiance to the Anglican Church prevented him from taking even
further radical steps. For example, Wesley did not allow lay preachers
to administer the sacraments, and he expected all members of the
classes to attend the Anglican service on Sunday. He did not apply
the doctrine of the priesthood of believers when he commissioned
his lay preachers.[20] Wesley constantly grappled with the tension
between his dual commitments: to the Scriptures and to the Church
of England. The bureaucratic structures within the Anglican Church
could not keep pace with the revivals and radical views Wesley
applied in his ministry. Wesley considered Methodism to be a reform
movement within the Anglican Church. However, his well-intended
directives to his followers to stay within the Anglican Church caused
a paradox between what he professed and what he practiced. Despite
his extraordinary innovations, the Anglican Church did not expel
Wesley; but, after his death, his approach eventually led to a schism
within the Anglican Church. The Methodist system of classes,
bands, and societies disintegrated, and what eventually surfaced was
a church with an organizational leadership structure very similar to
the Anglican Church. A few other reasons for these smaller cells or
teams closing were the increased affluence of Methodists, the larger
numbers within the classes, and the lack of interest in pursuing
holiness or perfection. One of the main reasons for the class
meetings' demise was the rise of stationed pastors who took over the

---

19   Snyder, *The Radical Wesley and Patterns of Church Renewal*, 74.

20   Snyder, *The Radical Wesley and Patterns of Church Renewal*, 100, 155.

responsibilities of class leaders.[21] The office of pastor came into effect only after Wesley's death, when the Methodists were left as "ecclesiological orphans," as the Anglicans did not endorse Wesley's mission efforts.[22]

It is beyond the scope of this book to recount the ways these various nurturing teams—classes, bands, societies, traveling preachers—changed society, but the Methodist emphasis on team-based discipleship offers a compelling model for cultivating Christ-centered teams today. However, reflecting on Wesley's journey reveals a vital lesson: Although structure is important, fully empowering emerging leaders and allowing new, organic forms of community to flourish—without the expectation of continued rigid adherence to traditional church attendance—is crucial for a truly transformative movement.

TEAMS in Methodism

Early Methodism, even among the uneducated, demonstrates how Wesley's approach to organizing everyone into various types of teams could aid transformation and revival. It showed that the spiritual health of believers depends on their active participation within a team of individuals who are intent on pleasing God. Early Methodism also demonstrated how God's people, activated by his Spirit, can mature in their faith as they take increasing responsibility for their own discipleship and disciple-making. Leaders were not expected to give lectures or lessons to the classes, bands, or select societies; but they helped with coordination and modeling Christlikeness. Traveling preachers periodically visited and encouraged the various groups and teams, but the groups were not dependent on them. Let's examine how the aspects of teaching, evangelism, adoration, mentoring, and sharing were incorporated into the structures of early Methodism.

---

[21] Snyder, *The Radical Wesley and Patterns of Church Renewal*, 175.

[22] Snyder, *The Radical Wesley and Patterns of Church Renewal*, 151.

Teaching: Mutual edification within the classes, bands, and societies, apart from the periodic visits of traveling preachers, helped foster a commitment to teaching. Teaching or preaching didn't occur only when John Wesley visited the area. Neither were they dependent on the traveling preachers alone; they learned from one another. This happened through a blend of dialogue, discussion, and pulpit preaching.

All these forms of learning are important. Sadly, some current initiatives tend to discount one form in preference of another. For example, a disciple-making movement (DMM) practitioner once told me that to encourage a participatory approach, they had forbidden preaching altogether. Maybe this approach was appropriate for a while, in order to cultivate a more participatory method of studying the Bible. However, rather than an either-or approach—*either* preaching *or* discovery—it may have been more appropriate to adopt a both/and approach—*both* discovery on a week-by-week basis *and* periodic preaching when all the teams gathered in a particular region—so that both methods were used in synthesis.

Wesley was known as a master synthesizer, and his approach seems to provide that balance. He employed all forms of learning, whether through monologue or dialogue approach, and they complemented each other. We need not discount one method over another. A seasoned pastor who visited one of our home churches found the discussions laborious. When he made a negative remark about these discussions to one of our newer members, we had to reaffirm the truth that a participatory approach was designed to facilitate active listening, rather than a passive approach to learning.

Evangelism: The tradition during Wesley's time was that sermons were to be preached within the confines of a church building. However, Wesley courageously broke through the expected norm and preached wherever he found opportunity among ordinary people. He also trained and released traveling preachers to do the same. Thousands responded to the proclamation of the gospel. The Methodist classes were yet another avenue for people to share their newfound faith with one another.

Adoration: Praise and prayer were practiced within all the various teams. The teams' small size provided an opportunity for everyone to praise God and share prayer needs, including confidential ones. Larger gatherings were not practical or conducive to accommodating everyone's prayer concerns or testimonies.

Mentoring: Wesley's personal involvement with the traveling preachers and the appointment of leaders in classes provided an atmosphere of mentoring within early Methodism. The mutual accountability structures within the classes, bands, and select societies helped sustain godliness among members.

Sharing: The financial contributions made through the various groups helped to support the traveling preachers and those in need. These contributions also aided various humanitarian efforts among the community at large.

The various functions practiced in these teams were one of the reasons that waves of revival broke out in Europe and North America.

Sparking TEAMS

Like the early Methodists, we can observe that the early followers of Christ in Acts 2 enthusiastically made efforts to grow in their commitment to Christ (Acts 2:36–47). As Christ's disciples, we can mature in our faith when we practice these functions consistently together as TEAMS. Considering how to implement this today raises several questions, including: Should a disciple-maker be an experienced follower of Christ, or can a new believer start up a team of Christ-followers? What about those involved in a legacy church? Can they go ahead and start up a group? Should they inform the leadership? What happens if the church leadership opposes and shuts down the idea? What about an underground movement in a hostile political environment? Should it be an underground movement within a church denomination or a local church itself? What are the ramifications for these groups if their leaders operate without a firm grasp of the foundational truths of the gospel?

These are questions many of us will have to grapple with, but interestingly, Christ also dealt with similar issues during his three years of ministry. It would be beneficial for us to first read the Gospels and closely observe how Christ started and motivated his team of disciples.

Below, I have unpacked a few frequently asked questions. The underlying principle in any situation or phase in life is to be sensitive to God's leading as he confirms his way when we seek him in prayer.

How do I initiate a team of disciples within a legacy church/ denomination? During the time of the New Testament, despite the existing religious system with the temple structure of Pharisees and teachers of the Law, God providentially prepared the way through John the Baptist. Christ's first few disciples emerged from John's team of disciples who were anticipating the Messiah. So, as you seek the Lord, remember that God will be the one to orchestrate events and prepare people to join you. You don't need to wait until you gather a large team; you can begin small, even with one person or their household.

Exercise wisdom and patience before challenging established practices. For example, if you are in a denomination or a church setting where communion is viewed as a sacrament officiated by the clergy, it may be unwise to immediately take communion at an early stage of your team meetings. Instead, you could begin by focusing on other biblical truths together or reading through the Gospels.

There may come a time when you have to courageously take steps to confront some of the existing practices within your denomination that may not be scriptural. However, remember that Jesus' approach to rebuking the existing religious structures came after years of preparation, as his ministry only began when he was around thirty years of age. Before directly confronting the system, prioritize developing a clear understanding of Scripture and deep communion with God. This takes significant time.

If you are in leadership within a legacy church or in a denomination, consider how you might innovatively apply many of the

TEAMS' principles. Once again, everything should be done with a humble attitude, as God leads and directs you.

If a person is new to faith or comes from another faith background, can they start a team? Consider the example of the Samaritan woman after she encountered Jesus by the well. Many other Samaritans believed in Jesus because of her testimony (John 4:39). She did not approach them as a scholar or one who knew it all but as an inquirer, evidenced by her questioning invitation ("Could this be the Messiah?" John 4:29). She engaged with those in her town as a fellow seeker on a journey of discovery. The town jointly came to a consensus declaring that "this man really is the Savior of the world" (John 4:42). Likewise, being a new believer or coming from another faith background should not deter anyone from starting a team. Regardless of our background, we should all adopt a posture of humility and learning.

Can we entrust new believers to be disciple-makers when they are still unclear of the gospel or unsure of God's ultimate purpose? Again, let's take a closer look at the way Christ worked with the Twelve when they were still far from understanding his purpose. Jesus entrusted the Twelve (Luke 9:1–6) to go in twos and talk about the coming kingdom even though they were far from understanding God's kingdom of peace. James and John wanted to call fire from heaven (Luke 9:54). Thomas didn't know "the way," even after spending three years with Jesus (John 14:5). And even after Christ had risen, he had to call out the disciples' foolishness on the Emmaus Road: "How foolish you are, and how slow to believe all that the prophets have spoken!" (Luke 24:25–26). Despite the disciples' clear shortcomings and limited understanding, the example of Christ entrusting the Twelve in Luke 9 to announce the coming kingdom and the subsequent response of the people illustrates how we should entrust new believers. The planned follow-up in Luke 10, where Christ intended to visit these same places and "fill in all the gaps" through his Word, reassures us that disciple-making by those still learning is part of a larger process where Christ himself brings deeper understanding. (And, remember, we are *all* still learning, so this applies to us all!)

This can reassure us that both new and mature believers serve as forerunners to declare the coming King, as long as we intentionally point people to Christ rather than depend on our own knowledge or experience. Later, Paul had to confront Peter to his face even though Peter had received the Holy Spirit, because Peter was not applying the truth of the gospel among the Gentiles (Gal. 2:11–21). Despite all the obvious weaknesses of the Twelve, Christ entrusted them with his Great Commission, and they matured along the way with God's Holy Spirit. Therefore, we can do the same if there is a willingness to learn and an openness to stand corrected in the light of Scripture and of God's conviction, which is available through the Holy Spirit and through our interactions with other fellow believers.

When God's Spirit indwells a person, an innate desire to grow closer to God prompts them to take responsibility for their own spiritual growth. Christian leaders need to foster and encourage this involuntary yearning to learn and mature in Christ, rather than making themselves the sole authorities to dispense insight and knowledge. The subsequent chapters provide guidelines for ways these functions can be voluntarily practiced by teams of two to a maximum number of twelve to fifteen members, without the aid or over-dependence on trained or professional leaders. Once again, each individual or team would need to prayerfully consider what would best fit their own context. Remember, disciples cannot be mass-produced. The disciple-maker needs to be aware of the realities in their local context and the season of life a person may be in. God celebrates diversity and creativity, and the principles in the following chapters can be reflected even as we learn, pray, and share life with one another. Creating a system or a method is helpful, as the early Methodists did; however, when there is an undue emphasis on methods over listening to God in prayer, things can disintegrate. Even sociologists are apprehensive of "McDonaldization"; likewise, we mustn't prioritize our methods over the message.[23] We need God's wisdom and to exercise discernment as disciple-makers.

Try It Out

Below are a few practices to help you rethink church in your context.

- **Study how Christ worked with teams:** Read Luke 8–10, where you can observe the "MAWL principle" at work. MAWL, an acronym for Model, Assist, Watch, Launch/Leave, is a core concept for disciple-making movement (DMM) trainers to describe reproducible principles for equipping new disciples to make disciples.

  Luke 8 illustrates Jesus' *modeling* ministry for the Twelve. In Luke 9, Christ *launches* the Twelve into independent ministry. After their return, he *assists* and *watches* them by offering instant feedback and underscoring the cost and privilege of discipleship as they served together. The phases of MAWL often occur concurrently in Luke 9. Jesus then applies this same approach with the Seventy-Two, *launching* or *leaving* them to serve on their own and supervising their efforts upon their return.

- **Form a team/teams:** Regardless of your current role—whether you lead within a church or organization or you're a new believer from a different background—prayerfully consider how you can form a team/teams if you haven't already. Discuss how you can grow and serve together by putting this book's principles into practice.

- **Evaluate TEAMS:** If you part of a team already, evaluate your current practices individually and collectively. Consider

---

23   Ashley Crossman, "McDonaldization and Why Sociologists Are Not Lovin' It," ThoughtCo., June 27, 2024, https://www.thoughtco.com/mcdonaldization-of-society-3026751.

how well you're integrating the TEAMS principles (teaching, evangelism, adoration, mentoring, and sharing), guided by the examples in Acts 2 and Early Methodism. Discuss specific ways you can proactively spur one another on to encourage each other's growth and your collective impact.

Meditate and Discuss

Reflect on what the following verses reveal about church.

- "Now if we are children, then we are heirs—heirs of God and co-heirs with Christ, if indeed we share in his sufferings in order that we may also share in his glory" (Rom. 8:17).
- "For we are co-workers in God's service; you are God's field, God's building" (1 Cor. 3:9).
- "Don't you know that you yourselves are God's temple and that God's Spirit dwells in your midst?" (1 Cor. 3:16).
- "Now you are the body of Christ, and each one of you is a part of it" (1 Cor. 12:27).
- "And God placed all things under his feet and appointed him to be head over everything for the church, which is his body, the fullness of him who fills everything in every way" (Eph. 1:22–23).
- "Consequently, you are no longer foreigners and strangers, but fellow citizens with God's people and also members of his household, built on the foundation of the apostles and prophets, with Christ Jesus himself as the chief cornerstone" (Eph. 2:19–20).
- "He is before all things, and in him all things hold together. And he is the head of the body, the church; he is the beginning and the firstborn from among the dead, so that in everything he might have the supremacy. For God was pleased to have all his fullness dwell in him" (Col. 1:17–19).
- "But Christ is faithful as the Son over God's house. And we are his house, if indeed we hold firmly to our confidence and the hope in which we glory" (Heb. 3:6).

 **Any Questions?**

 **Any Ideas?**

 **Anything That Touches Your Heart?**

6

TEACHING

*I used to think that the amplified and distant voice of the
sage on the stage was most reliable. But I've come to learn the
timely still small voice of the guide on the side, who knows me
and my situation, is far better.*

IN 2002, GOD had opened the door for me to contextualize and
record Vernon McGee's "Thru the Bible" (TTB) series for Trans World
Radio (TWR-India). While recording messages from the book of
Galatians, I invited an acquaintance, Jeff Imam—who had a Muslim father
and Catholic mother—to join us for weekly home gatherings. We were
working through Galatians, using McGee's notes as a guide. Recognizing
Jeff's limited exposure to many of the Old Testament concepts addressed
in Galatians, we approached the guide in an unhurried manner. Eight
months later, Jeff realized the need to surrender his life to Christ. Through
this group, Jeff experienced true fellowship, prayer, and a passion for
sharing Christ. One night he brought a suicidal woman he had just met.
My wife, though apprehensive, shared the gospel and offered counsel, and
the woman returned home with renewed hope and courage.

In 2005, these experiences and the connections we had built
with Jeff led us to plant "Radiance"—a new church in the outskirts of
Bangalore at Whitefield. Our aim was to focus our attention on those

working at call centers. For two years, we held church services in a designated building following a conventional format—with a pulpit, expository sermons, and a worship team. Though we made some connections and saw some results, we soon realized our teaching model needed to revert to the original approach we had used with Jeff— giving people a chance to discuss the Word with others and engage in prayer and fellowship. Over time, our groups began to multiply, and we saw firsthand people being transformed as they experienced a more participatory way of studying and discussing God's Word.

Radio Homes

While all this was taking place in Whitefield, I continued to record TTB programs for TWR. As a result, I ended up interacting with George Phillip, who at the time (2006–2007) was one of the state directors. He had been contemplating an economical way to engage with teaching— encouraging listeners to study God's Word apart from the medium of radio. He desired a model where fellowship could also be integrated. His preference had always been a form of church that was "self-admin- istered, self-propagated, and self-supported, which was autonomous in nature."[1] Recognizing our common desire for the church to be simple and reproducible, I shared Radiance's story—how it transitioned from a conventional church to a network of home churches. After visiting one of our gatherings and engaging in continued discussions and mutual sharing of resource material, George eventually conceptualized Radio Home Groups. He first applied them in Gujarat. TTB's website states,

> A Radio Home Group is simple: Gather 7–10 people every week
> to listen to Dr. McGee's teaching on a digital player, followed by
> discussion and prayer. The hope is that this group would eventually
> develop into a church fellowship.[2]

---

[1]   George Phillip, Personal Interview, February 2014.

[2]   "From Home Groups to Churches: The Gospel Travels a New, Old Path," Thru the Bible

After George Phillip became CEO of TWR in 2010, the experience and success of Radio Home Groups in Gujarat prompted him to train leaders to adopt this strategy across the country. As of 2025, there are more than seventeen thousand Radio Homes in India alone, using this simple but powerful teaching idea. On seeing the phenomenal results in India, TTB began to adopt this approach all over the world, motivated by one of McGee's statements years earlier:

> The church has never been the building. Many of the great mausoleums called churches today are nothing but a pile of brick and stone and mortar. The real church is a living body of believers.[3]

God divinely orchestrated the emergence of Radio Home Groups through various relationships, partnerships, and resource materials provided by individuals and organizations.

Learning About Teaching Through the Journey of TWR and TTB

Many people associate the word "teaching" with an image of a qualified Bible teacher speaking from a pulpit. Or they think of a set curriculum at a discipleship camp, a seminar, or a book. While these can be helpful, effective discipleship involves more than merely downloading and absorbing biblical content.[4] Instead, it involves ensuring that people *obey* the truth. The goal should be obedience-based discipleship, not knowledge-based discipleship. We see this described in the Great Commission: *"teaching them to obey everything* I have commanded you" (Matt. 28:20, emphasis mine).

---

with J. Vernon McGee, accessed October 6, 2022, https://www.ttb.org/global-reach/home-groups.

3   "From Home Groups to Churches."

4   John Koessler, *True Discipleship: The Art of Following Jesus* (Chicago, IL: Moody Publishers, 2003), 155.

Christ turned everyday life situations into teaching moments for transformation. David Watson, known for conceptualizing disciple-making movements (DMMs) states,

> Disciples must be made or formed—not just informed as the church has tended to do for so long…. Imparting information is not enough … we must share our lives with one another to such a degree that God is able to share His life in and through us.[5]

This chapter delves into the teaching component of TEAMS, examining the importance of shifting from a model of authoritative dissemination to a more nuanced, relational approach.

The story of TWR-India and TTB, and my subsequent involvement, illustrates this necessary transition. TWR was founded in 1952 with a vision to utilize mass communication for evangelism. By January 1956, TWR's impact was already evident, with broadcasts reaching forty countries in twenty languages.

In the mid-1960s, William Paul Mial, a TWR-International staff member stationed on the small Caribbean island of Bonaire, heard a sermon that challenged him to consider the vast, unreached populations of the world—specifically the two-thirds of the world that had yet to hear the gospel. Mial dedicated his life to serving and loving the Indian people by ensuring the broadcasts were spoken in the heart languages of the people.

TWR-India's launch of Thru the Bible (TTB) in several languages in the early 1980s amplified their commitment to contextualized teaching. TTB was originally a recording of Dr. Vernon McGee's sermons for US Radio stations.[6] McGee's folksy storytelling approach, alongside his exposition of the Bible from Genesis to Revelation, made this a very popular program. TTB eventually consolidated

---

[5] Watson, *Discipleship*, 83.

[6] "Dr. J Vernon McGee," Thru the Bible, accessed October 6, 2022, https://ttb.org/about/dr-j-vernon-mcgee.

these sermons into a five-year Bible study series and facilitated local Bible teachers, through agencies such as TWR-India, to translate and adapt these messages for specific audiences across diverse cultural contexts. Effective teaching often involves taking foundational content and making it relevant and accessible to specific audiences. My own involvement, in being asked to adapt and narrate these messages for the average English-speaking Indian audience and eventually leading to the concept of Radio Homes, further exemplifies this contextualized approach.

Today, TWR-India broadcasts sound Bible teaching in 150 languages across several platforms, including radio, television, and YouTube. This isn't simply about broadcasting more content; it is about ensuring the message resonates deeply by being delivered in a language people truly understand. This contextualization is a cornerstone of relational teaching, acknowledging the audience's specific needs and cultural framework. TWR-India's subsequent establishment of fifty-six audience relation centers across the country further solidified this shift, embodying the relational aspect of teaching, which recognizes that discipleship is nurtured through ongoing connections and personalized guidance rather than passive reception of information. These centers move beyond one-way communication, playing a vital role in providing follow-up support to interested listeners.[7]

The evolution of TWR and TTB in India provides a compelling example of moving beyond a purely authoritative model of teaching. The success in reaching seventeen thousand groups was not solely due to the initial broadcast reach but rather by fostering genuine, transformative discipling relationships by intentionally shifting toward contextualization, language accessibility, building connections, and offering personalized engagement that truly connected with and empowered learners. Those seventeen thousand groups could not

---

7 Word Resounds Today, "About," accessed May 13, 2025, https://www.wrtoday.org/about-us.

have been achieved had it not been for the volunteers, listeners, staff, and founders who served sacrificially in obedience to God's call.

TEAMS Teaching Principles

The teaching aspect of TEAMS can take many forms. There is no one single approach to studying the Bible. It can be an amalgamation of various methods, with the intent of learning and applying Scripture. The following are some principles and intentional steps to foster a commitment to God's Word in our approach to teaching.

Journey with a Small Group of Individuals

As we explored in the first half of this book, Jesus' discipleship process involved serving with a team of twelve; he concentrated his efforts on a few key people. Christ's example of concentrating on a few "illustrates a fundamental principle of teaching: that other things being equal, the more concentrated the size of the group being taught, the greater the opportunity for effective instruction."[8] Following Christ's example of focusing on a few, we can enhance the teaching aspect of TEAMS by journeying with a small group of individuals. This approach allows for in-depth Bible study and discussion, enabling people to grasp the truth for themselves and fostering a culture of discipleship rooted in obedience. The intimate nature of a smaller group provides crucial accountability, increasing the likelihood that action plans derived from studies will be implemented. This fosters a culture where team members can challenge and support one another in practicing the principles they have read or studied together, leading to genuine transformation. Below are some useful sites to help with personal Bible studies or aid groups in studying together.

- Inductive Bible Study[9]

---

8   Coleman, *The Master Plan of Evangelism*, 26–27.

9   "How to Study The Bible," Navigators, accessed May 13, 2025, https://www.navigators.org/resource/how-to-study-the-bible/.

- Discovery Bible Study Method[10]
- SOAP Bible Study Method[11]
- Swedish Bible Study Method[12]
- SPECK Bible Study Method[13]

The challenge is not so much who facilitates or how the discussions take place, but whether the truth is obeyed. The team's main objective is to foster a culture of obedience to the Scripture rather than merely having a good discussion. While this can be incorporated when the team meets together, it also involves interacting with one another informally beyond the time of the actual Bible study—whether that is through WhatsApp threads, in-person meet-ups, or Zoom calls.

Don't Mistake Information for Reformation

Whatever Bible study method we choose, we need to incorporate a way to evaluate whether we are truly obeying God's Word. It's not just about completing a class or a curriculum. This involves relational discipleship, where the discipler closely observes their disciples' lives and responses. Incorporating "iron sharpening iron" discussions (Prov. 27:17) gives everyone the opportunity to share honestly about whether they consistently followed through with spiritual disciplines or how they responded to various life situations.

---

[10] "Discovery Bible Study: A Safe place to see for yourself what the Bible says," dbsguide.org, accessed February 12, 2024, https://www.dbsguide.org/.

[11] "SOAP – Easy Bible Study Method (Individual Or Small Group)," My Salvos Toolkit, accessed February 12, 2024, https://my.salvos.org.au/toolkit/resource/easy-bible-study-method---soap--individual-or-small-group-method/624/.

[12] Tim Challies, "Faith Hacking: The Swedish Method," challies.com, September 1, 2014, https://www.challies.com/christian-living/faith-hacking-the-swedish-method/.

[13] Patrick Mabilog, "Here's a simple Bible-reading format you can follow," Christian Today, April 28, 2016, https://www.christiantoday.com/news/heres-a-simple-bible-reading-format-you-can-follow.

Embrace Spirit-Led Disciple-Making

Disciple-making is a profound journey of transformation, requiring much more than intellectual engagement. It cannot be done in an hour of teaching, reading, or even studying the Bible together. It necessitates time and the empowering presence of the Holy Spirit. It involves emulating a Christlike lifestyle modeled by a leader, a process best embodied in coaching and apprenticeship. This approach embraces learning or teaching in the context of failure, experimentation, and growth. (We will look at this in more detail in the chapter on mentoring.) The twelve disciples often struggled to fully comprehend Jesus' purpose, despite their close proximity to him, their direct witnessing of his power and authoritative teaching, and their experience of learning alongside him. Some of the disciples doubted even after the resurrection (Matt. 28:17). It wasn't until the coming of the Holy Spirit that they eventually understood the significance of their calling and mission. The power of God's Spirit is essential for people to assimilate and apply truth. This process cannot be rushed or rely solely on human efforts.

Cultivate Active Discernment

Beyond structured learning in the form of curricula and programs, we must cultivate a culture of active discernment, encouraging individuals and groups to glean truth for themselves from the wealth of available resources. Today, there is an abundance of information available at our fingertips, whether in written form, audio, or video content. While the Bible remains central, we can guide people to valuable supplementary materials, appreciating the contributions of Bible colleges and online courses. Some home church practitioners discourage believers from listening to online sermons or attending a Bible college. However, we need a balanced perspective—we needn't be dependent on the qualified or belittle those who have no theological foundation, but we can still receive the wisdom from experienced theologians who can help us stay true to the gospel.

Navigate Educational Opportunities

As resources multiply and people receive additional education, we must acknowledge that those who are motivated may pursue opportunities to gain knowledge elsewhere. There will always be a risk of losing local witnesses when people leave their home environments to pursue higher Christian education. Due to this risk, disciplers have discouraged or even prevented those eager to pursue Christian education in a nearby city or overseas. But we must be careful about this. God may be preparing that self-motivated disciple to be a voice on a global scale. Although there is much debate on this issue, it's undeniable that the movement of people across borders for better prospects in all fields is a reality today, more than ever before. Let's not forget that, in part, it was the apostle Paul's Roman citizenship and his credentials from Tarsus that enabled him to have considerable influence across the then-known world. And his Jewish heritage gave him access to Jewish audiences in the synagogues across the Roman Empire.

In our pursuit of obedience-based discipleship, we've explored various teaching methods, emphasizing that true spiritual growth transcends mere knowledge acquisition. Although cultivating a culture of participatory Bible study and fostering good discussions are essential, this does not render other forms of communication or resources obsolete. Ultimately, spiritual formation occurs not through the passive reception of information but through the active practice of truth. The teaching element of TEAMS, therefore, must aim beyond intellectual understanding, guiding believers to embody the principles of Christ in their daily lives.

Try It Out

Below are a few practices to begin incorporating teaching in your TEAMS.

- **Experiment with one of the Bible study methods listed on pages 86–87:** Write down your observations, interpretations, and, most importantly, your planned actions for obedience. Be specific and measurable if possible. For example, instead of "be more loving," write, "I will intentionally listen without interrupting to one person each day this week."
- **Try an "obedience challenge":** After a Bible study, encourage the group to identify one specific action point based on what they learned and commit to practicing it during the week. The following week, they can share their experiences and discuss the challenges they faced.
- **Focus on modeling Christlike character:** Encourage disciplers to prioritize living out the principles they teach, recognizing that their example is a powerful form of instruction.

Meditate and Discuss

Reflect on what the following verses reveal about teaching.

- "Be sure to keep the commands of the Lord your God and the stipulations and decrees he has given you. Do what is right and good in the Lord's sight, so that it may go well with you" (Deut. 6:17–18).
- "Keep this Book of the Law always on your lips; meditate on it day and night, so that you may be careful to do everything written in it. Then you will be prosperous and successful" (Josh. 1:8).
- "The law of the Lord is perfect, refreshing the soul. The statutes of the Lord are trustworthy, making wise the simple. The precepts of the Lord are right, giving joy to the heart. The commands of the Lord are radiant, giving light to the eyes" (Ps. 19:7–8).
- "Great peace have those who love your law, and nothing can make them stumble" (Ps. 119:165).

- "Heaven and earth will pass away, but my words will never pass away" (Mark 13:31).
- "Consequently, faith comes from hearing the message, and the message is heard through the word about Christ" (Rom. 10:17).
- "Let the message of Christ dwell among you richly as you teach and admonish one another with all wisdom through psalms, hymns, and songs from the Spirit, singing to God with gratitude in your hearts" (Col. 3:16).
- "Therefore, get rid of all moral filth and the evil that is so prevalent and humbly accept the word planted in you, which can save you. Do not merely listen to the word, and so deceive yourselves. Do what it says" (James 1:21–22)

 **Any Questions?**

 **Any Ideas?**

 Anything That Touches Your Heart?

EVANGELISM

I used to think the gospel was merely a one-time password to heaven. But I increasingly realize that it is an ongoing privilege to serve as kings and priests of God's kingdom here on earth, right now.

POOJAPPA LIVED IN Goramadagu, about 44 miles (71 kilometers) from Bangalore, in a very remote area on the border of Andhra Pradesh. Poojappa means "man of worship"—"Pooja" means "worship," and "Appa" means "father," which can also be used in a respectful way to address an older man. (I am sharing the meaning of this and other individuals' names to highlight the fascinating alignment between their names and the responsibilities they ultimately fulfill.)

To this day, Goramadagu lacks proper roads, public transportation, and government high schools. The area was founded about two hundred years ago by five families who sought refuge from a deadly plague. Over time, the village grew as many others settled in the area.

Poojappa was born into a low-caste tribe known as Madigas, who were historically tanners and artisans, but are now often involved in agriculture. Typical of many Indian villages, lower-caste families are not permitted to reside within the village premises, nor are they allowed to draw water from the village well. Though there are government programs to uplift the downtrodden, many accept this impoverished way of life as their fate. Poojappa was never allowed inside the homes of the landlords or those from higher castes. After he surrendered himself to Christ through the efforts of a Christian mission agency from Kerala, Poojappa did not hold back his enthusiasm and love for Christ, even though he was an uneducated, illiterate outcast.

A family of Gowdas, a higher caste, employed Poojappa as a daily wage worker to assist with their lands and do other menial tasks around the house. Under the shade of a tree, Poojappa was known to share stories and songs of Christ with fellow workers during lunch. Srinivas, one of the sons from this family, fondly recalls how in the late 1980s, Poojappa would often sit by their doorstep when they were doing their homework. Poojappa would ask Srinivas and his siblings to read stories from his New Testament. After several years, Srinivas's brother Obanna, along with his wife, became believers and got baptized, but they kept it a secret for almost three years. Poojappa faithfully followed up with Obanna and continued to motivate him by meeting with him under the tree on their farm and sharing what he had learned. Eventually, the other children followed suit and gave themselves over to Christ as they saw the evidence of God's peace and joy in Obanna's family and through Poojappa's example. They also saw that the gospel was offered at no cost, without the need to appease any gods by offering poojas or sacrifices. However, Srinivas and Obanna's parents were apprehensive about making any open commitments.

Srinivas's parents refused to allow their children to attend any of the church gatherings in Poojappa's home due to village and caste customs. That didn't stop Poojappa from relaying stories and songs on the farm or by their doorstep. When Srinivas's parents eventually came to faith, age-old beliefs and strongholds began to gradually fall, as God's peace and salvation took root in this Gowda family, much to the consternation of the village elders. Despite mounting opposition and segregation from village community life, Srinivas's family chose to follow Christ wholeheartedly and took radical but gradual steps to remove idols and images of gods and goddesses. They also stopped participating in temple festivals, processions, and offering money for religious rituals. Caste barriers continued to linger, and they avoided going to Poojappa's home, but they welcomed Christian workers to their own home for weekly prayer meetings. These workers were affiliated with the mission Poojappa was associated with. Excited about having these weekly meetings in their home, the family invited relatives, workers, and friends from the neighborhood. Manohar, the mission's worker assigned to their area, shared the creation story with them. ("Manohar" incidentally means "one who wins over the mind.")

The meeting that began outside under the trees evolved into a weekly gathering at Srinivas's parents' house, and several other evangelists and Bible teachers regularly taught the Scriptures. This home became a lighthouse, a missional base for the village. Many surrendered themselves to Christ and were transformed. Over a considerable length of time, strongholds and preconceived ideas began to crumble. They began to host lower-caste families in their home. They shared their water, food, and drink, which was further evidence of the gospel's impact on their lives. It didn't stop there—Poojappa, Obanna, and Srinivas began to share the gospel in other homes in the vicinity and later to surrounding villages. During this time, they finally visited Poojappa's home—the power of the gospel demolishing the stronghold of casteism.

Another Christian worker from the mission agency—Devadas, whose name means "servant of God"—had a profound impact on the family, especially the children and young people who attended the meetings. He inculcated the importance of education and encouraged them to explore the world beyond their village. Many parents subsequently encouraged their children to pursue education, even if it meant walking 4.5 miles (7 kilometers) to the closest school and 10 miles (16 kilometers) to the nearest college. Srinivas testified with much gratitude that from this small village church of about ten families, eight individuals committed themselves to study in a Bible college, six became nurses, and several became teachers or lawyers. Srinivas eventually initiated a network of home churches and started his own window cleaning business. Today, there are approximately sixty groups reaching the neighboring state. Recently, around fifteen believers from these groups became actively engaged in Bible translation into their local dialect. From the proceeds of their window cleaning business, they were able to build a facility, which serves as a multipurpose hall and is used for worship and teaching on Sundays.

Poojappa's life was sadly cut short by an epileptic seizure, leaving behind his wife and three young children. However, he left a legacy of faithful followers who continue to serve the Lord in many places to this day. Although he was uneducated and considered an outcast, he began a chain reaction of transformation simply by being a faithful witness. The people of Goramadagu witnessed the first-ever Christian funeral service when Poojappa was respectfully buried and honored by the higher caste families—an act which previously would have been unimaginable. This became another testimony of the power of the gospel and the hope of eternal life. Whenever he recounts his testimony, Srinivas always acknowledges Poojappa's faithfulness, which not only transformed his family but also several communities in the area. Amazing things can happen when people discuss and learn about the gospel in their home fellowships and seek to apply God's Word. As they intently study the Scriptures, spiritual leaders are formed, who can make disciples and spread the gospel.

TEAMS Evangelistic Principles

Poojappa's life demonstrated the practical application of TEAMS evangelistic principles. Below are some approaches we can adopt for effective gospel sharing.

Make Love Foundational

Poojappa's love for God could not be contained. His love for Christ superseded his limitations, such as his inability to read or write and the constraints imposed on him by society due to his caste status. None of these barriers curtailed his yearning to share the truth. In fact, his inability to read became the gateway through which he kindled an interest among the family he worked for, and especially their children. Moreover, his consistency in singing and sharing stories of the God he loved eventually brought about a breakthrough. The gospel wasn't communicated in a few minutes; it took years for the family to make any significant changes. He didn't base his commitment to evangelism on seeing quick results but rather on his love for Christ and his neighbors.

Evangelism should not be just an activity done for a few hours on the weekend, but rather an effervescent lifestyle of God's love flowing through us. Our words should contain glimpses of the things Christ said and did that can spark an interest in people to further seek the truth (1 John 1:3). It should be a natural overflow of our heart, not merely a scripted summary of the gospel message, with a cute diagram or illustration. This is especially so when sharing with people from other faith backgrounds. Too often, well-meaning Christians, in their zeal to evangelize, proclaim the gospel without building a loving relationship, without listening or observing, and without knowing the individual's complex background. We need to observe, listen, and maintain relationship with people, irrespective of their response, while sharing truth progressively and consistently. Diagrams or illustrations can be helpful, but only when used as part of sharing the story of Christ, undergirded by an exemplary Christlike lifestyle.

Keep Evangelism in the Context of Discipleship

Poojappa simply focused on sharing stories of Christ's life, coupled with his godly example and faithfulness; and over time, the seed of the gospel came to fruition. Discipleship happened, possibly even without Poojappa or the children being aware of this concept.

Alan Hirsch emphasizes the fact that the Great Commission does not refer to evangelism but rather to discipleship. He stresses the importance of Christ-followers intentionally focusing on the discipleship process, even before a person from another religion comes to saving faith or realizes Christ's lordship. He points out that conversion, the conviction of sin, and even the breaking of various bondages are all God's work. The believer's responsibility is to consistently share with others the reality of Christ and the implications of what it means to follow him: "Evangelism is implied in the process of disciple-making and not the other way around. Discipleship is evangelism's true context."[1]

Notice Poojappa initiated discipling relationships even before anyone surrendered themselves to Christ. Poojappa had unconsciously accomplished what Hirsch described: "We can simply focus on discipling people, weave our narratives into theirs, live the kingdom life, and make space for God to do his thing in giving them new life in him."[2]

Poojappa was intentionally and relationally focused on the circle of influence God had entrusted to him. It took years before Srinivas's family took steps to commit themselves to Christ. Poojappa's approach did not provide instant results or decisions, but his perseverance eventually brought about lasting fruit and transformation.

People from another faith can begin to grow as disciples as they fellowship with the church community, during which time the gospel gradually takes root in them, bringing about transformation. Therefore, evangelism, discipleship, church, and leadership formation can take place simultaneously. The implications and the depth of their understanding will grow, provided people make the effort to obey when prompted by God's Spirit.

Unfortunately, many Christians compartmentalize these aspects as if they were stages to be accomplished in a linear fashion rather than growth points that can be incorporated simultaneously throughout life.

---

[1]   Alan Hirsch, *Disciplism: Reimagining Evangelism Through the Lens of Discipleship* (Cody, WY: 100 Movements Publishing, 2024), 8.

[2]   Hirsch, *Disciplism*, 13.

> We need to reconceive discipleship as a process that includes
> pre-conversion discipleship and post-conversion discipleship. A
> person's salvation really is God's business, isn't it? Our part in it
> is to simply devote meaningful time and commitment to making
> disciples of whoever wants to share the journey with us—as we go.[3]

Notice how evangelism, discipleship, church formation, and leadership took place simultaneously in Poojappa's story. Despite his limitations of not being able to read or write, Poojappa served as a leader among his fellow workers and among his employer's children, by the doorstep. He hosted the church in his home and, along with other believers, influenced Srinivas's family. We don't see clear demarcations between evangelism, discipleship, church life, and leadership. While Poojappa himself was being saved and growing in faith, he was serving actively in the field. Likewise, in Srinivas's family's case, they began meeting as a church even before they fully grasped the truth that the gospel does not differentiate people based on class or caste. Srinivas was evangelizing the neighborhood with songs before he could articulate the gospel in words or even pray. Speaking of Jesus' activity in the Gospels, Hirsch says, "All the while, [Jesus is] just discipling them along the way, until the gospel narrative finally weaves its way into their hearts, and they come alive to God in new birth."[4]

When we observe how Jesus helped the disciples to mature in their faith, we can see that growth as a disciple took place in all areas simultaneously. The concept of church wasn't fully realized until Pentecost, but Christ inculcated principles of what it meant to be his body, the church, during his lifetime. He trained the Twelve to eventually advance and sustain his vision with the power of God's Spirit. As noted in an earlier chapter, Jesus authorized the disciples to baptize, preach, and cast out demons as fellow leaders and kingdom-workers

---

[3] Hirsch, *Disciplism*, 17

[4] Hirsch, *Disciplism*, 14.

even while they were still in the process of understanding the significance of his purpose on earth. It is the Holy Spirit who brings about change over the course of time. Therefore, those excited about the person of Christ may invariably motivate others even while they are still taking time to apply the implications of the gospel, such as discarding idolatry, casteism, or superstition. We need to trust God to bring about change at the opportune time, which can take several years. As Hirsch points out, this is something we are all experiencing:

> Discipleship is the process of assimilating the gospel, done over a whole lifetime, into the whole of our lives. In a very real sense, we are all still being evangelized (Phil. 1:6; 2 Cor. 3:18, etc.). Evangelism is an aspect of discipleship, and discipleship is an aspect of evangelism—and it's all about Jesus.... They are in effect two sides of the same coin.[5]

Avoid the Mission-Compound Approach

When Poojappa became a follower of Christ, he continued to serve under the established traditions of the village, even though those traditions were unfair. Obanna continued to stay on within the higher caste Gowda community, choosing to hold back from immediately declaring his faith. Their patience and perseverance eventually won several families over to Christ, and the subsequent transformation in various areas of their lives drew the attention of the whole village.

The goal of evangelism is not to produce personal decisions but to mobilize the whole community for Christ by working through the family. It is therefore unwise to prematurely celebrate an individual's conversion or put pressure on them to declare their personal decision immediately, or to disciple a new believer beyond their local context and expect them to attend a brick-and-mortar church or even a gathering among other believers from another community.

---

5   Hirsch, *Disciplism*, 23.

In the past, mission agencies extracted individuals from their own communities and formed Christian communes within a mission compound. The mission-compound approach of extracting new believers from their own communities can put undue pressure on a new believer to join a particular congregation. All sorts of Bible verses could be used to encourage them to cut ties with their family. This may be necessary at some point, but it's wiser to ensure a whole family, a household, or a good number of people within a community have the opportunity to come to faith through the first believer. In a community-oriented society, it is always better to wait for a joint communal response rather than prematurely celebrating one personal decision for Christ.[6]

In Luke 10 and Mathew 10, we read that Christ instructed his disciples to first serve in and through the home of the "person of peace." When that person welcomed them, it tended to open a door to acceptance by the whole community. Christ did not ask the disciples to recruit people to come alongside them, nor did he instruct them to establish a separate community in the vicinity.

In first-century Palestine, people lived in clans within their allotted tribal areas, connected geographically and socially. Therefore, the person of peace became the gateway to the whole community. In an urban context today, we cannot assume that a person of peace has influence over a geographical area or even among their families. They may provide access to a social group (which could include their families) that is virtually linked across geographical and ethnic borders. While this offers great potential, it also requires navigating significant cultural complexities. For example, a software professional in India may be connected with people residing in the US, Japan, or China. Though they may be well-connected on a professional level, the lack of physical proximity, coupled with varying religious and cultural

---

6   David Watson and Paul Watson, *Contagious Disciple Making* (Nashville, TN: Thomas Nelson, 2014), 112.

beliefs, could be a challenge when a follower of Christ attempts to share his/her faith.

In Obanna's case, the whole family responded to Christ because of his sensitivity and wisdom. Christ calls for wisdom: "Be as shrewd as snakes and as innocent as doves" (Matt. 10:16). Hasty declarations of faith without sensitivity to the local context can often be detrimental to the kingdom.

The mission-compound approach, or forming a holy huddle of Christians, can minimize effective inroads into the community. It is therefore imperative to incorporate the need to interact with unbelievers, to live and share life "like lambs among wolves" (Luke 10:3). An exemplary lifestyle of humility in the community while gently introducing Christ through conversations will eventually convict and draw people to him by God's Spirit.

Make Methods Secondary

When considering ways to reach out to Hindus, well-meaning Christian mission agencies (often Western) have marketed creative tools to share the gospel, on the premise that a simple sharing of the gospel is all that is needed to fulfill our role in bringing Jesus to Hindus. In his book *Disciple Making Among Hindus*, Timothy Shultz, who has thirty years of experience in this area, disagrees with this approach and goes on to state that it is in fact unbiblical.[7] Creative tools are good, but we shouldn't become fixated on them. In the process of promoting these tools, the gospel message is sometimes reduced to a bracelet, rope trick, diagram, or five-minute presentation that focuses on heaven and the afterlife. It ignores the depth and commitment that discipleship demands. The implications of what following Christ involves and how the gospel has the power to break strongholds remain unclear.

---

[7]   Timothy Shultz, *Disciple Making Among Hindus: Making Authentic Discipleships Grow* (Pasadena, CA: William Carey Library, 2016), 37, www.missionbooks.org.

Creative and innovative methods have helped thousands, perhaps millions of people, to get an overview of the gospel. Yet they may not be sufficient for people of other faiths to grasp the truth, as they hold a different worldview. For example, the ideas of a monotheistic God, sin, or eternal life are foreign concepts to Hindus. Therefore, it is better to explain foundational truths starting from Genesis than merely presenting facts about Christ through a diagram or a page. Our primary source of inspiration should be God, who will prompt us to say and do what is unique and most appropriate for that person or group.

The need for God's people to be devoted to him and to serve or speak only at his bidding should supersede methods. Methods or tools often promoted from the West can easily overshadow the value of indigenous people who are living epistles, such as the Poojappas (men of worship), the Manohars (those who win over the mind) and Devadases (servants of God) who plant, nurture, and harvest the seed of the gospel over several years. Their method may never be reproducible. The way Christ dealt with Zacchaeus (Luke 19:1–10) was quite different from the way he interacted with the Samaritan woman (John 4:1–42). Rather than latching onto a method, we need to stay in tune with God's Spirit. He will prompt us to say or do the right thing, which may (or may not) include using a tool that helps us to share the gospel.

When we seek to devote ourselves to evangelism, we need to incorporate times of waiting and prayer as Peter did in Acts 2. He courageously declared the hope of salvation at the opportune time, after much prayer and in the power of the Spirit. A commitment to evangelism requires spending sufficient time with people, helping us to understand their context by first listening to them and observing the challenges they face. The gospel can be shared at the right time, accompanied by prayer for God's miraculous intervention, and while we engage in compassionate service. Quick and easy marketing strategies do not necessarily work for sharing the gospel. People from other faiths may resist such an approach and are more likely to receive and respond to a listening ear in the context of genuine friendship.

Try It Out

Below are a few practices to begin incorporating evangelism in your TEAMS.

- **Study how Jesus trained the disciples to become fishers of people (Luke 9:1–9, Luke 10:1–24) and apply the principles learned:** The disciples' ability to proclaim the good news was rooted in their initial and ongoing surrender to Christ. Take note that they proclaimed the good news only *after* they had surrendered everything to follow Christ (Luke 5:11). They were appointed to focus only on one household within a region. The gospel was not intended to be a brief encounter. They were to go with nothing except a prayer on their lips that the Lord would send workers. This meant they were not to be overly "burdened" by the problems that existed in the various towns or homes they visited; the real issue was often the halfhearted followers of Christ (Luke 9:57–62). Upon reaching a home, they were to first enjoy the host's hospitality (Luke 10:7), and while interacting with the family, pray for the miraculous to take place (Luke 10:9). It was only after enjoying the food, which incidentally wasn't "fast food," that they were to share about the coming kingdom (Luke 10:9). This implies that there was considerable time spent getting to know the host family before any conversation about the kingdom took place. They were not expected to "blitz" the whole area or try to gather a large crowd to reach as many people as quickly as possible. Instead, they were instructed to greet no one on the way (Luke 10:4) or even attempt to share the good news with other travelers. The focus was only on one family (Luke 10:5–7).

- **Start where you are, with what you know, with who you know:** God has placed you among family members or a specific team at your workplace. Make attempts to connect with them in a humble manner, not with the hope of hosting them for a meal but rather with the hope of being invited for a meal, within their sphere of influence. Upon gaining an understanding of their context, culture, and real-life issues, pray for God's supernatural intervention at the opportune time. In due course, share your experiential understanding of God's grace at work in your life. As time progresses, and if the Lord wills, this could possibly become the team with whom you can implement the TEAMS principles.

Meditate and Discuss

Reflect on what the following verses reveal about evangelism.

- "Declare his glory among the nations, his marvelous deeds among all peoples" (1 Chron. 16:24).
- "The fruit of the righteous is a tree of life, and the one who is wise saves lives" (Prov. 11:30).
- "Let all the world look to me for salvation! For I am God; there is no other" (Isa. 45:22 NLT).
- "How beautiful on the mountains are the feet of those who bring good news, who proclaim peace, who bring good tidings, who proclaim salvation, who say to Zion, 'Your God reigns!'" (Isa. 52:7).
- "When you enter a house, first say, 'Peace to this house...' When you enter a town and are welcomed, eat what is offered to you. Heal the sick who are there and tell them, 'The kingdom of God has come near to you'" (Luke 10:5, 8–9).
- "However, I consider my life worth nothing to me; my only aim is to finish the race and complete the task the Lord Jesus has given me—the task of testifying to the good news of God's grace" (Acts 20:24).

- "For I am not ashamed of the gospel, because it is the power of God that brings salvation to everyone who believes: first to the Jew, then to the Gentile" (Rom. 1:16).
- "How, then, can they call on the one they have not believed in? And how can they believe in the one whom they have not heard? And how can they hear without someone preaching to them?" (Rom. 10:14).
- "We proclaim to you what we have seen and heard, so that you also may have fellowship with us. And our fellowship is with the Father and with his Son, Jesus Christ" (1 John 1:3).

 *Any Questions?*

 *Any Ideas?*

 Anything That Touches Your Heart?

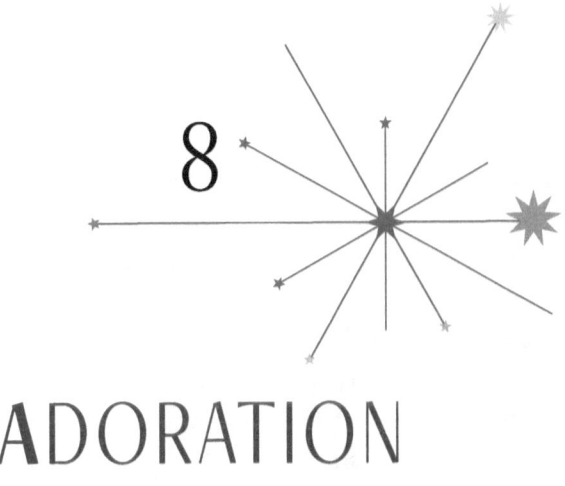

ADORATION

I used to think of worship as a time of songs, hymns, and exclamations of praise. But now I realize we need to also model quiet meditation and celebrating obedience to God's Word as worship.

DURING MY TEENAGE years in the 1980s, I recall that at every youth camp, our church youth leaders would hold a session where they pointed out that the use of musical instruments during worship was unscriptural. Though this is not a common belief among local fellowships of my denomination, surprisingly, it is a view that some local church congregations continue to hold to. This view obviously bewildered and agitated many of us musicians. The already existing generation gap widened further, and we were branded "young rebels." Some left the fellowship entirely, seeking more accepting church denominations. Others eventually started new fellowship groups elsewhere. I joined another church and found it refreshing to be able to worship God with instruments without being required to provide a theological explanation. At this time, similar debates were taking place in almost all churches about the use of electric guitars, drums, Christian rock music, choruses, praise and worship music, and other forms of contemporary Christian music. Many churches were divided over the issue. While young people questioned the status quo, older members were flabbergasted that the "Devil's music" had become a regular feature in their hallowed sanctuaries and cathedrals.

Given this background, you can imagine my surprise when, after one of our first home church gatherings, my mentor, Neill Mims, quite casually stated that I should avoid bringing my guitar to subsequent sessions. Given my earlier experience of the church's view on instruments, I wondered where the conversation would lead. I was relieved when he shared his reason. He told me that people would find it easier to grasp the true meaning of worship if I also practiced what I believed and taught. I believed and did teach that worship is not just about music, but at the time, my actions and regular practice did not reflect this. I used the guitar quite regularly whenever we spent time in corporate worship.

I then realized how I was unconsciously reinforcing the idea that worship only takes place when there is music. Neill also stressed the importance of keeping the gatherings simple and reproducible, so that the groups didn't become dependent on musicians. His suggestion that I should intentionally model other ways of worshipping God not only impacted me, but I also saw how writers and artists responded positively when we incorporated their creative art forms during times of corporate worship.

Neill's explanation brought to mind an incident that occurred in the church I had served in earlier and led me to reflect on how worship is understood. A few of the cell-group leaders seemed upset that their time of worship was weak because the cell-group coordinator had not assigned any musicians to their group. They concluded that the quality of their worship was dependent on musicians. Similarly, a simple Google search of the word "worship" revealed to me what worship means to the general populace: My screen was filled with several silhouetted images of worship bands on a stage with smoke machines and strobe lights, playing toward a congregation with uplifted hands. This "rock concert" approach would've been considered outrageous a few years ago. In many churches, contemporary worship has been reduced to a performance of music by trendy young people in praise bands. I don't discount the songs of worship or the impact they have had on this generation, but I fear our practice doesn't reflect what we profess: that worship is a lifestyle, ascribing worth to God by our obedience. We need to inculcate other forms of worship, especially in smaller group settings, to emphasize the value of obedience and a lifestyle of worship.

TEAMS Adoration Principles

In practicing TEAMS adoration, we've found the following ideas effective when a team of disciples comes to worship or pray together. I have incorporated prayer as part of adoration, recognizing that the very idea of us approaching God in prayer is a way of acknowledging that he is Lord over all.

Please note that many of the suggestions aim to foster a lifestyle of obedience through personal praise and worship. The idea is to encourage people to participate out of the overflow of God's presence in their lives. A lack of engagement or unedifying conversations may indicate the overall spiritual health of the group or of individuals, potentially signaling hurt or a lack of commitment to Christ. Group members should be sensitive to these signs of disengagement and actively encourage and disciple those who are struggling. (Remember, disciple-making should be the responsibility of every group member.) This can be done by listening to and praying with individuals in times outside of formal gatherings.

Be Respectful of the Worship Styles of Other Faiths

Online images of Muslim worship show men on their knees with their faces down, paying obeisance to Allah. Images of Hindus and Buddhists show people with clasped hands bowing down before their deities. They would consider it disrespectful to wear shoes in most, if not all, of these holy spaces. People of most Middle Eastern or Eastern religions tend to dress down or wear their traditional clothes during worship. The experience of a Western-influenced Christian worship service in a conventional church building, with mixed seating of men and women and varying dress codes, can therefore be overwhelming for many Hindu- and Muslim-background believers.

The point is not whether one is better than the other or whether one is right or wrong. However, we need to be aware that people of other faith backgrounds are accustomed to very different forms and styles of worship. Therefore, as we engage in our teams, it is unwise to hastily expect believers from other faith backgrounds to readily adopt our practices. It is important to be aware of their culture and practice and to adapt our forms of worship when making initial contact with a particular group or those who could serve as people of peace.[1] Imposing a form of worship that we are familiar with but that is insensitive to the local context can become a distraction or a hindrance. It may be more appropriate to use local instruments or ask people to write their own songs of praise. While remaining biblical, worship should be adapted to fit the cultural context rather than hastily inviting people to "our church," where rituals and practices can be quite alien (or Western) to them.

Practice 1 Corinthians 14:26

"What then shall we say, brothers and sisters? When you come together, each of you has a hymn, or a word of instruction, a revelation, a tongue, or an interpretation. Everything must be done so that the church may be built up" (1 Cor. 14:26).

Applying this verse within a team setting, which ranges from two to fifteen members, is doable and practical. However, this requires each member to be prepared to audibly worship the Lord. It assumes that every member is in tune with God throughout the week, and when they come together, they worship him out of the overflow of the Spirit at work in their lives. A person may contribute a song, read a

---

[1]   "People of peace" or "a person of peace" is used commonly to refer to people who gladly open their home or household to followers of Christ. This is based on Luke 10:1–10.

psalm, or share a revelation, a tongue, or an interpretation, as the verse suggests. While the primary objective is to worship God, whatever is shared should also edify the body or team. For example, if the group includes children or young believers, individuals should not use lofty and complicated theological terms in their sharing. It should uplift and edify everyone, and thus glorify the Lord. 1 Corinthians 14:26 calls for everyone to carefully and collectively weigh what the prophets say, since not every word spoken within the community is necessarily accurate.

A spontaneous time of worship may sometimes include awkward silences. These times of silence may help us collect our thoughts or focus on the Lord. However, they may also indicate a lack of spiritual vitality. This calls for honest conversation and an assessment of the church's spiritual health.

Write or Draw to Express Gratitude to God

Incorporating a time of observing nature before gathering can effectively center the group on the Lord. This practice—rooted in biblical truths like Psalm 19:1, Romans 1:20, and Job 12:7–10, where creation testifies to God's glory and power—is meaningful for both children and adults. Stepping outside the confines of buildings allows us to intentionally recognize God's handiwork. Upon assembling, participants can spontaneously share or show their reflections. In response, members might write a psalm, hymn, or spiritual song, expressing praise and thanksgiving to God. Similarly, sketching or drawing provides a creative way to offer thanks. This form of giving worth to God during the gathering encourages a habit of coming prepared to offer worship through individualistic artistic expressions.

Use Online Resources for Music

Lack of musicians within a group does not mean we need to forego music altogether. Online resources offer valuable accompaniment or can be useful when learning new songs. Additionally, listening to songs meditatively can be edifying.

Embrace Short Prayers

While extended prayer times are valuable, we should also embrace the frequent, opportune moments for brief, meaningful time to call out to God in prayer. These can be practiced individually or corporately and are easily adopted by younger believers. Below are a few suggestions.

Breath Prayers

These are short prayers based on Scripture, which can be recited within a single breath.[2] The idea is to meditatively reflect on a phrase while breathing and praying. I find them especially useful during long runs or walks, where the rhythm of my breath helps me meditatively verbalize these prayers. Breath prayers at dawn, while observing God's creation, are particularly reinvigorating.

Below are a few examples of breath prayers. I do not necessarily pray a whole verse in one breath, but I may repeatedly focus on one phrase before I proceed to the next. I may then periodically read through the whole passage to see the verse in context. These verses have a way of recalibrating my thoughts and my heart toward the Lord. Some verses are more like reminders or affirmations that serve as a motivation to persevere in faith.

- "Here I am, I have come—it is written about me in the scroll. I desire to do your will, my God; your law is within my heart" (Ps. 40:7–8). Based on this verse, I repeat the following phrase: "Here I am, I have come ... I desire to do your will, oh my God." At times, I quote the whole verse.
- "Do you not know that in a race all the runners run, but only one gets the prize? Run in such a way as to get the prize" (1 Cor. 9:24). "Run in such a way ... so as to win the prize" is a motivational chant, especially when I feel tired and want to

---

2   For more on breath prayers, see Jane E. Vennard, "The Breath Prayer," The Upper Room, accessed May 14, 2025, https://www.upperroom.org/resources/the-breath-prayer.

stop running. I use this opportunity to contemplate the need to persevere in my walk with the Lord and fulfill his purposes.

- "And God said, 'Let there be light,' and there was light" (Gen. 1:3). I pray, "Let there be light" when moving into a new territory or while walking by different areas as a prayer for God's light to shine through and bring about transformation.
- "Now go; I will help you speak and will teach you what to say" (Exod. 4:12). God's assurance, "I will help you speak … and teach you what to say [or do]" is an encouraging breath prayer, knowing that he will help me speak and accomplish his desires.
- "Show me your ways, LORD, teach me your paths" (Ps. 25:4). I recall and repeat these verses in prayer when I need God's guidance and direction.

Several verses from Scripture can be used in breath prayer. They can be practiced personally and incorporated when the team comes together.

Prayer Walks

Bob Pierce founded World Vision in 1950, based on a prayer he scribbled in his Bible after walking and being moved by the sight of an orphaned girl in South East Asia. The prayer was "May my heart be broken by the things that break the heart of God."[3] World Vision continues to help millions of vulnerable children across the world to this day.

To cultivate a similar heart of compassion, prayer walks offer a tangible way to engage with the needs of a community.[4] Prayer walks can easily be accommodated when a team gathers. They can be practiced even when a family is driving through a region or locality. The idea is to direct prayers to God as we identify needs in an area. For example, various buildings could prompt us to pray for the people who

---

3   "Our History," World Vision, accessed February 15, 2024, https://www.wvi.org/our-history.

4   For more information about prayer walks, see "Prayer Walk," Navigators, accessed May 14, 2025, https://www.navigators.org/resource/prayer-walk/.

reside in or frequent those buildings. A school building could prompt us to pray for the students and teachers. Seeing a government office may prompt us to pray for those who serve within. Observing people, such as those who are homeless or businesspeople in work attire, can give us an insight into a particular area; and we can respond by interceding with specific needs in mind. We may have walked or driven in certain places many times before, but these intentional prayer walks or drives help us to observe what's happening on a deeper level and identify needs that have always existed. This will change our perspective, and God may prompt us to serve those needs in some way.

The Ten2b Prayer Model

Two busy doctors came up with the idea of two individuals committing themselves to pray for two minutes at 10:02, based on Luke 10:2: "Ask the Lord of the harvest, therefore, to send out workers into his harvest field." God hears the shortest of prayers offered sincerely.[5] To foster consistent prayer in your team, encourage designated prayer times throughout the week, such as 10:02, for individuals or small groups to focus on mission-related requests. You might consider using digital reminders and providing prayer prompts to maintain focus, creating a team culture of brief, powerful prayer.

Incorporate Silence and Contemplation

Quiet contemplation, meditation, and prayer are absent or minimal in many modern worship services. We have lost the art of being still and taking things at a slower pace. As teams, we need to relearn what it means to intentionally quieten our hearts to hear God, above the noise, the rush, and the drive to be engaged in various activities, including Christian endeavors. How many times have we caught

---

[5] "10:2b Prayer," LK10, accessed November 29, 2022, https://lk10.com/tag/102b-prayer/.

ourselves reaching for our phones when we have a few moments of waiting in an elevator or a queue?

The Quakers are known to wait in silence, even within a group setting, until someone is prompted by God's Spirit to speak. Prayer is not only about talking *to* God but also talking *with* him and hearing what he has to say. Therefore, when we gather, we may have to intentionally create times of silence so we can align ourselves with God and his Spirit before we begin to hear his voice. The people of God, whether in the New Testament or the Old Testament, consistently called out to God for guidance, especially before they attempted any new venture. God's guidance may override our experiences, plans, and strategies. It is best to seek him rather than place our confidence in human beings' suggestions, strategic plans, methodologies, or principles, even when laid out in the best of books. In *Celebration of Discipline*, Richard Foster explores the value of solitude and silence in depth.[6]

Try Lectio Divina

This is an ancient form of reading the Bible slowly and meditatively.[7] In a group setting, a facilitator guides participants through the following four or five steps, reading and leading the reflection to foster deep spiritual insight.

Preparation: After introducing the idea of lectio divina, the facilitator gently guides the group to quieten their hearts. Participants should be seated in a comfortable posture, preferably with eyes closed, away from distractions and noise. To achieve a sense of stillness, with a sense of anticipation of hearing the Lord's voice, this practice often requires time. Therefore, the facilitator may need to guide the group with many pauses, encouraging them to release distractions, conflicting thoughts, and to-do lists, to cultivate an expectant heart.

---

[6] Richard J. Foster, *Celebration of Discipline*, Revised 1988 (New York, NY: HarperCollins Publishers, 1978).

[7] "Lectio Divina: An Ancient Contemplative Spiritual Practice," *faithward*, accessed May 9, 2025, https://www.faithward.org/lectio-divina-an-ancient-contemplative-spiritual-practice/.

Reading/listening: When there is a sense of stillness within the room, the facilitator can proceed by reading the passage which he/she has prayerfully chosen beforehand. The passage should not be too lengthy and should be read very slowly, with many pauses. The passage should be repeated two or three times. After each reading, the facilitator shares instructions, requesting participants to identify words, phrases, or ideas that caught their attention.

Meditation: During this phase, the facilitator reiterates the request for individuals to reflect on the word, phrase, or idea that captured their attention and relate it to a current situation they may be facing. The facilitator also reminds the participants to surrender to God any conflicting thoughts or pressing needs. There should be an unhurried time of quiet contemplation as people meditate on the phrase or word that caught their attention.

Prayer: The facilitator encourages people to pray about their situation and praise God for how the word, phrase, or passage ministered to them.

Share: After this time of personal prayer, members within the group can share with one another how the Lord ministered to them through the passage, phrase, or word.

All these suggestions are ways teams can pray or praise together. True adoration is more than words that we sing or pray at a designated time and place, following traditional rituals. Instead of considering worship as a musical set—three up-tempo songs and one or two slower meditative songs, led by professionals—we should also incorporate joyful expressions from the overflow of our hearts, resulting from obeying God. True worship of God involves trusting and obeying him, living by faith through his power. We need always to have an attitude of worship during our everyday routines and to ensure that we surrender our heart, will, and mind to God's sovereign control.

Try It Out

Below are a few practices to begin incorporating adoration in your TEAMS.

- **Practice the above suggestions together:** Experiment with different approaches to implementing the above suggestions for corporate times of praise or prayer. Consider going through the practices in this chapter and trying out a new suggestion each time you meet. Or you could focus on one of the methods for several weeks and gain a good understanding and application before moving on to a new idea. Alternatively, try out some of these suggestions either as individuals or with one other person, and then share your experiences when you all gather together.
- **Ask each member to share how they have exercised obedience throughout the week:** When you gather, ask each individual to share how they chose to obey God or even failed to obey God through their week. This exercise not only creates a culture of accountability but also reinforces the truth that worship is about giving worth to God by our everyday acts of obedience. Rather than being judgmental, the team needs to function as a support group to encourage or spur one other on. Depending on what members share, it may either prompt the group to rejoice and praise God for their accomplishments, or it may provide an opportunity to intercede for one another in prayer.

Meditate and Discuss

Reflect on what the following verses reveal about adoration:

- "But Samuel replied: 'Does the Lord delight in burnt offerings and sacrifices as much as in obeying the Lord? To obey is better than sacrifice, and to heed is better than the fat of rams'" (1 Sam. 15:22).
- "If my people, who are called by my name, will humble themselves and pray and seek my face and turn from their

wicked ways, then I will hear from heaven, and I will forgive their sin and will heal their land" (2 Chron. 7:14).

- "Hear my cry, O God; listen to my prayer. From the ends of the earth I call to you, I call as my heart grows faint; lead me to the rock that is higher than I" (Ps. 61:1–2).
- "I remember the days of long ago; I meditate on all your works and consider what your hands have done" (Ps. 143:5).
- "This is what the Sovereign LORD, the Holy One of Israel, says: 'In repentance and rest is your salvation, in quietness and trust is your strength'" (Isa. 30:15).
- "Also, seek the peace and prosperity of the city to which I have carried you into exile. Pray to the LORD for it, because if it prospers, you too will prosper" (Jer. 29:7).
- "After they prayed, the place where they were meeting was shaken. And they were all filled with the Holy Spirit and spoke the word of God boldly" (Acts 4:31).
- "And pray in the Spirit on all occasions with all kinds of prayers and requests. With this in mind, be alert and always keep on praying for all the Lord's people" (Eph. 6:18).

 *Any Questions?*

 Any Ideas?

 Anything That Touches Your Heart?

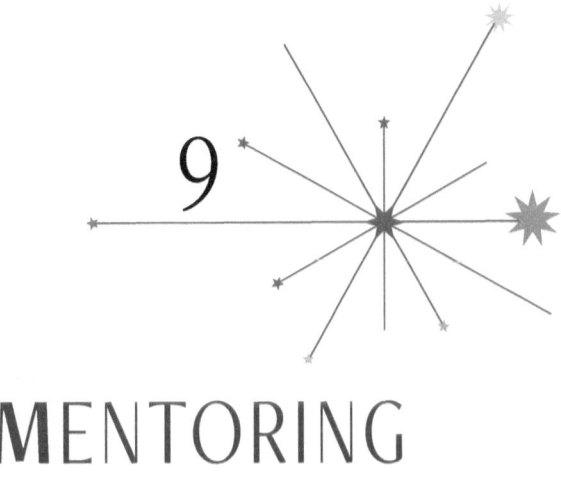

MENTORING

I used to believe that mentoring depends on the mentor's intellect or abilities, but now I appreciate that effective, Spirit-led mentoring involves deflecting attention away from ourselves and redirecting people to listen to the Lord's voice.

MANY ARE FAMILIAR with Paul's *missionary* journeys, but Paul's *mentoring* journey—which took place simultaneously with his missionary trips—is just as significant. He never acted as a lone ranger. Instead—mirroring Christ's model described in part one of this book—Paul constantly drew, influenced, and empowered his fellow team members while they reached out to those who hadn't yet heard the gospel.

Before his conversion, Paul (known at the time as Saul) went against his mentor, Gamaliel. He lobbied for an aggressive campaign against the followers of Christ, even beyond Jerusalem (Acts 22:3–5). On gaining the high priest's consent in writing, Paul then got on the road like a snorting bull, breathing murderous threats to imprison Christ's disciples until, while he was enroute to Damascus, God's light brought him down to the ground (Acts 9:1–3).

This strong-willed, ambitious young religious ruler, who was determined to exterminate the believing community, was now blind and helpless and had to be led by the hand. Having gone without food or drink for three days, he was on his knees praying fervently when God prompted a disciple named Ananias to visit and pray for his healing. The temporary blindness and the resulting uncertainty were God's mentoring tools to prepare Paul for the journey ahead. After years of obscurity—which included being in the desert and serving as an unsung hero—Paul was eventually taken under Barnabas's wing, with them subsequently serving together. However, this partnership was short-lived, and they parted ways. Despite this seeming setback, Paul continued the practice of mentoring.

Paul's travels and ministry environments provided ample opportunities for him to mentor young men such as Silas, Timothy, Titus, and other team members. His letters served as an additional mentoring tool for his team while they served in different locations. Mentoring did not take place in closed offices or monasteries but on dangerous roads and in troubled waters. Paul emulated the way Christ mentored his disciples, as he used the fields, the trees, and the crowds, and responded to circumstances as opportunities to drive home important lessons.

Though mentoring and discipleship are closely linked, they are not synonymous. If we consider discipleship to be the way Christ worked with the Twelve, mentoring is the way he focused his attention specifically on Peter, James, and John (Matt. 17:1; Mark 5:37; Mark 14:33).

Mentoring thrives in the context of real life rather than through one-on-one sessions, following a set curriculum, or reading a book. Mentors leverage God-ordained events, observations, and experiences to inculcate principles, values, or truths that provide direction. Shared activities—such as sport, ministry, or a work environment, or navigating challenging environments like overcrowded, noisy Indian roads—offer practical mentoring opportunities. These environments reveal a person's true nature, in contrast with formal settings, where mentees can present a curated image to impress their mentor.

TEAMS Mentoring Principles

People generally gravitate to human mentors because of their ability, giftedness, or personality. However, Christlike mentoring points people to God and his Word. Consider an usher at an event: A good usher discreetly leads visitors to their seats without disturbing the performance. John the Baptist did the same. He was intentional and proactive in pointing people to Christ, knowing that Christ must increase while he himself must decrease (John 3:30). Likewise, we too need to intentionally serve in the background, pointing people to God and his Word as quickly as possible—just as Christ, John, Paul, and the other apostles did. If not, our educational qualifications, background, experiences, gifts, or talents may inadvertently draw people's attention to ourselves instead of highlighting God and his Word.

In practicing TEAMS mentoring, we've found the following principles can help us value and apply mentoring effectively.

Embrace God as the Ultimate Divine Mentor

The idea of mentoring is popular today, whether in business or matters of spirituality. While this has led many to proactively seek out mentors, it can often lead to a sense of inadequacy when human mentors are hard to find, or it is difficult to relate honestly to them. Although God uses human mentors, they can never replace or compare with God. He is more than enough. God is far superior; he is just, good, loving, steadfast, reliable, and trustworthy. The divine Mentor not only has the power but also yearns to communicate and reform his people.

The apostle Paul fled to Arabia, partly due to a threat on his life, and stayed for three years, where Christ enlightened his understanding of the gospel.[1] He intentionally chose not to consult any other human, including the apostles in Jerusalem. Instead, he chose to have Christ alone as his divine Mentor. He wrote,

---

[1] "Why, When, and For How Long Was the Apostle Paul in Arabia?" Got Questions, accessed April 25, 2025, https://www.gotquestions.org/Paul-in-Arabia.html.

I want you to know, brothers and sisters, that the gospel I preached
is not of human origin. I did not receive it from any man, nor was I
taught it; rather, I received it by revelation from Jesus Christ.

GALATIANS 1:11–12

But when God, who set me apart from my mother's womb and
called me by his grace, was pleased to reveal his Son in me so that I
might preach him among the Gentiles, my immediate response was
not to consult any human being. I did not go up to Jerusalem to see
those who were apostles before I was, but I went into Arabia. Later
I returned to Damascus.

GALATIANS 1:15–17

Paul chose to pursue God rather than place his confidence in human
beings. He did not replace Gamaliel with Peter; neither did he strive
for a position of power by associating himself with the other apostles.
He intentionally chose to be with God alone for a considerable length
of time until God directed him to meet the apostles.

The three years of obscurity and silent years of ministry in Cilicia
and Syria were all part of the process of mentoring. God's revelation
during that time shaped Paul's understanding of the gospel, then
prompted him to approach those who were leaders (Gal. 1:11–12;
2:1–2). Even though fourteen years of silence and obscure service are
glazed over in a verse or two, we should not discount or underestimate
the reformative power that obscurity and solitude can bring about.
Human mentors can never replace what God the Father orchestrates
and accomplishes. We need to cherish our God-ordained hidden and
silent years. They are precious experiences, foundational to our fruitfulness and our faithfulness to him, especially when we do not see
results and our efforts seem futile.

God is far more concerned with character formation than
merely changing external behaviors. He is intent on ensuring that
we are reformed from the inside out. Our access to Christ, knowing
that he deals gently with the weak and ignorant, shows how God

mentors his people through Christ (Heb. 4:15–16; 5:2). The Holy Spirit's presence, offering advocacy, comfort, and counsel in times of need, is far superior to any human source of help, regardless of how professional or educated it may be (Rom. 8:26–27; John 14:16–20; John 14:26).

Once Paul had established his own relationship with God, he was ready to help others do the same. He understood the importance of life-on-life examples and went on to mentor many individuals.

Use Scripture as a Reliable Source for Mentoring

In addition to the Triune God, his written Word is an infallible guide. The psalmist proclaims "the Law of the LORD is perfect, refreshing the soul" (Ps. 19:7). Its reliability and transformative power are constantly highlighted throughout Scripture.

> He has given us his very great and precious promises, so that through them you may participate in the divine nature.
>
> 2 PETER 1:4

> For everything that was written in the past was written to teach us, so that through the endurance taught in the Scriptures and the encouragement they provide we might have hope.
>
> ROMANS 15:4

In his instructions, guidance, and correction, even Christ repeatedly drew people's attention to God's Word rather than himself alone. For example, when the two disciples were distraught on the road to Emmaus, Jesus could have quite easily convinced them that he was indeed alive. He could have revealed himself to them in the flesh, but we read that their eyes were intentionally closed. Instead, Jesus chose to open their minds, and their hearts burned within them as he explained about himself from all of Scripture (Luke 24:13–32). We need to point people to the Word, instead of drawing attention to our knowledge, insight, or experiences. Those being mentored need to discover the truth for themselves and reflect who they ought to be in the light of God's Word, rather than becoming clones of their mentors.

Take a Team Approach to Mentoring

The early church consisted of participatory communities that gathered in homes around the table for fellowship. This provided a natural environment for mutual edification and encouragement. Mentoring and discipleship took place quite naturally, during informal times of conversation while they dined together (Acts 2:42–47; 1 Cor. 14:26–33). Many churches default to a model where services are perceived as a well-coordinated event centered on what happens on stage, relegating the congregation to the role of passive spectators. Edification and exhortation might happen *informationally*, but a close-knit community is essential for spurring one another toward action and personal transformation (Heb. 10:24–25). Therefore, the church, when gathered as a team, can very naturally provide that environment for mentoring. However, developing trust, transparency, and vulnerability within a group requires time together and intentionality.

Be Aware that Mentoring Is Messy

Jesus and Paul had many disappointments as they mentored their disciples. Despite years of teaching and modeling humility and service, Jesus was troubled by the request of James and John's mother for seats of honor for her sons. Similarly, Peter's impulsive act in cutting off a soldier's ear and later denying Christ show that mentoring does not guarantee immediate transformation. Paul experienced the messiness of mentoring when everyone deserted him, with Phygelus and Hermogenes even turning away from (2 Tim. 1:15).

An investment of time and effort in mentoring people offers no guarantee that those being mentored will remain our friends for life. Mentoring involves risk and can be painful. But as we depend on God and mature in the faith, God enables us to spot reliable people, to pass on what has been entrusted to us.

In his mentoring commission to Timothy—"the 222 principle" (2 Tim 2:2)—Paul does not assure or promise Timothy material blessings, accolades, or praises; he calls him to join him in his struggle.

> You then, my son, be strong in the grace that is in Christ Jesus. And the things you have heard me say in the presence of many witnesses entrust to reliable people who will also be qualified to teach others. Join with me in suffering, like a good soldier of Christ Jesus.
>
> 2 TIMOTHY 2:1–3

Solitude, obscurity, and the challenges inherent in mentoring may seem daunting. However, if we are to see longevity and fruitfulness in ministry, we must follow Christ's example. He called and appointed a few to be with him. He commissioned them to preach and to have the authority to expel demons (Mark 3:13–15). These simple, uneducated men set the world aflame with God's love through his Spirit. Christ's focus on the few required him to withdraw from the masses. We read that he did not entrust himself to the crowds, even though they believed in his name: "But Jesus would not entrust himself to them, for he knew all people. He did not need any testimony about mankind, for he knew what was in each person" (John 2:24–25).

Investing time with the Lord and his Word will provide us with the wisdom and discernment needed to identify reliable individuals. They can, in turn, carry out his mission while identifying other trustworthy people who can do the same and pass on the truth, no matter the cost.

Try It Out

Below are a few practices to begin incorporating mentoring in your TEAMS.

- **Seek God about mentoring:** Just as Paul was led to approach the apostles before he was given the "right hand of fellowship" (Gal. 2:1–10),[2] seek the Lord about whom you can approach to obtain their blessing, by way of mentoring. However, this assumes that you are in close communion with the Lord, and you are reading his Word regularly. If this is a practice you are struggling with, you may want to identify an accountability partner or a team who can help you instill the habit of hearing God through his Word.

- **Seek out people to mentor and journey with:** Just as Barnabas sought out Paul, and Paul later identified a team to journey with him, be prayerfully intentional about finding people with whom you can closely work so they can grow closer to the Lord and do the same with others. Remember, this process will be riddled with challenges and disappointments, just as Paul faced these things when he had to part ways with Barnabas over John Mark's decision (Acts 15:36–41). However, in the long run, the practice of mentoring, as recorded in 2 Timothy 2:2, will be rewarding and well worth it.

Meditate and Discuss

Reflect on what the following verses reveal about mentoring.

- "These commandments that I give you today are to be on your hearts. Impress them on your children. Talk about them when you sit at home and when you walk along the road, when you lie down and when you get up" (Deut. 6:6–7).
- "One generation commends your works to another; they tell of your mighty acts. They speak of the glorious splendor of your majesty—and I will meditate on your wonderful works" (Ps. 145:4–5).

---

[2] See "What is the right hand of fellowship (Galatians 2:9)?" Got Questions, accessed May 14, 2025, https://www.gotquestions.org/right-hand-of-fellowship.html.

- "As iron sharpens iron, so one person sharpens another" (Prov. 27:17)
- "But the Advocate, the Holy Spirit, whom the Father will send in my name, will teach you all things and will remind you of everything I have said to you" (John 14:26).
- "Whatever you have learned or received or heard from me, or seen in me—put it into practice. And the God of peace will be with you" (Phil. 4:9).
- "For the Word of God is alive and active. Sharper than any double-edged sword, it penetrates even to dividing soul and spirit, joints and marrow; it judges the thoughts and attitudes of the heart" (Heb. 4:12).
- "And let us consider how we may spur one another on toward love and good deeds, not giving up meeting together, as some are in the habit of doing, but encouraging one another—and all the more as you see the Day approaching" (Heb. 10:24–25).
- "Be shepherds of God's flock that is under your care, watching over them—not because you must, but because you are willing, as God wants you to be; not pursuing dishonest gain, but eager to serve; not lording it over those entrusted to you, but being examples to the flock" (1 Pet. 5:2–3).

 *Any Questions?*

 *Any Ideas?*

 *Anything That Touches Your Heart?*

10

SHARING

I used to think sharing depended on an abundant supply of resources. But now I know that our reliance on God's grace will enable us to share spontaneously, sacrificially, and joyfully.

SAROJ SUBBA COMES from a remote and rugged mountainous region in the Himalayas of West Bengal. He comes from the Gurkha Nepali community of the Limbu tribe.[1] His religious upbringing was primarily defined by his mother, who worshipped nature and Hindu gods and goddesses. In the year 2000, as a seventeen-year-old, questions of life after death prompted him to eventually surrender himself to Christ as he conversed with a Christian friend. His faith grew considerably as they interacted, read through the Bible, and served in the local church. Saroj enjoyed attending various short-term Bible schools and seminars. In 2004, he married Bandanna Rai and became a father by the age of twenty-two.[2]

The Gurkha community—found in Sikkim, Nepal, and West Bengal—is renowned for its men's courage and physical fitness. This

---

[1]   Travel Log, "Limbu/Limboo Documentary from Sikkim India," YouTube, July 28, 2018, https://www.youtube.com/watch?v=v7elPxOJnuI.

[2]   Bijaya Limbu, "Traditional Village Marriage System of the Nepal, Limbu Culture, Bijaya Limbu," YouTube, March 5, 2022, https://www.youtube.com/watch?v=aDphCVHCDdU.

reputation has led both the Indian and the British armies to establish Gurkha regiments, recognizing their bravery and effectiveness in combat. Those who do not qualify for a place in the army generally opt for jobs in nearby cities because farming in the terraced mountainous region is hard manual labor with minimal returns.

Despite all the honorable and revolutionary options ahead of him, Saroj chose to study at All Nations Theological Seminary in Siliguri. In October of 2006, during a casual college annual picnic beside the Teesta River in Mong Pong, God began to place a calling on Saroj's heart. Saroj initiated a conversation with some of the children who lived on the riverbank. "Something seemed very special about this meeting," says Saroj, which prompted him to take note of the children's names.[3] On returning to college, he couldn't shake off the burden he felt for the children. However, he didn't dwell on the idea as he was a long way from graduation, and his daughter was only a few months old.

On revisiting Mong Pong, he learned that many of the parents were concerned about the inherent dangers involved in their children accessing nearby education. They shared about a road accident that had occurred while a mother and aunt were taking their child to the neighboring school. The mother was instantly killed, and the aunt was left with lifelong injuries. Health issues and several other tragedies, such as wild elephants on a rampage, were added concerns that made them anxious about sending their children to school. Deeply moved by their struggles, Saroj began tutoring students free of charge on weekends and mobilized his friends to join him.

Along with tutoring, Saroj integrated himself into village life and helped the men with construction and farming. He taught children to sing and play the guitar and joined them while they played in the evenings. All these activities provided a gateway for Saroj to share stories of Christ. He distributed literature and cassettes with gospel

---

[3]   Rai Saroj, Zion School, personal interview, February 16, 2023.

messages in the Limbu language, with only one old man showing interest. On meeting Saroj the following week after listening to sermons in his own heart language, the old man exclaimed, "Jesus is a Limbu!" He had concluded that Jesus was a Limbu because he had heard and read the gospel in the Limbu language. The old man became one of the first followers of Christ in the village. A kind elderly mother responded to the gospel as well and hosted Saroj whenever he was delayed and unable to return home for the evening. By the end of 2007, Bandanna, Saroj's wife, relocated to Mong Pong with the couple's two-year-old daughter.

In January of 2008, Saroj and Bandanna officially opened Mount Zion School in Mong Pong, with ten children. It gradually grew, as more children joined from surrounding areas. Over time, several young people came to faith and were among the first ones to get baptized in 2009. Many others came to assist in the work, including teachers, well-wishers, and financial supporters. By God's grace, Saroj was able to purchase the land and build classrooms. In 2010, they opened a boarding facility because some of the children could not trek through rough terrain daily. In 2017, a few of us visited Saroj and Bandanna to conduct some training on the value of Christians meeting together within homes. We were deeply moved by their dedicated service.

Saroj shared with us that, after experiencing the challenges of living in a remote village in the hills, the thought of an easier life in the city was alluring. He told us that the 2020 COVID-19 pandemic proved to be a challenge. Funds were depleted, and everything seemed to be imploding. A disgruntled parent made a false charge that Saroj was forcibly converting people, which got him into trouble with the local authorities. Despite all these challenges and the mounting hardship, Saroj and Bandanna persevered. During the pandemic, they became more intentional in encouraging church members to gather in their own villages and homes.

Today, six vibrant home churches meet in neighboring villages, along with a larger gathering of approximately ninety people, who meet in the school chapel every Sunday. Three hundred and twenty children are studying in the school, of which seventy are boarders. Despite the surrounding pressures, Saroj and Bandanna embody a lifestyle of contentment and generosity, sharing with others what God has given them.

TEAMS Sharing Principles

In practicing TEAMS sharing, we've found the following principles can help us share our lives, money, resources, time, and effort with others.

Share From God's Grace

Saroj and Bandanna's lives illustrate the grace of God, similar to the apostle Paul's description of the Macedonian church (2 Cor. 8:1–5). He commended them for the way they gave to the famine-stricken church in Judea. They gave joyfully beyond his expectations, even giving beyond their means. Note the motivation behind their incredible generosity:

> We want you to know about *the grace that God has given the Macedonian* churches.... They *gave themselves first of all to the Lord,* and then by the will of God also to us.
>
> 2 CORINTHIANS 8:1, 4, emphasis mine

True generosity results from a deep relationship with God. It is not merely the result of human effort or sympathy but rather the outpouring of God's grace, channeled through disciples who have surrendered to him.

In Acts 4:34, we read that God's grace was so powerfully at work in the early church that there were no needy persons among them. When God's people focus on cultivating a deep relationship with God and choose to seek his will, they will naturally be inclined to give sacrificially and cheerfully.

Share Life and Discern Needs

Sacrificial giving and service emerge from a shared life where individuals are vulnerable enough to reveal their personal needs. The early church's practice of meeting together in homes, in small groups, facilitated transparency and vulnerability, enabling people to both easily discern and share needs, whether physical, emotional, or spiritual (Acts 2:44–45; 4:33–35).

Share Through Openness and Transparency

A practical way to encourage openness and transparency is to use a tool such as SASHET.[4] It helps everyone within a group to identify and articulate how they are presently feeling. The acronym SASHET stands for Sad, Angry, Scared, Happy, Excited, and Tender.[5] Everyone picks one or a combination of these emotions and then shares how they are faring in life. Depending on what is shared, the others can rejoice, pray, or weep with them.

Share Life Stories

Sharing one's life story can be a great bridge builder. This can be done informally as people get to know one another or incorporated into regular gatherings. Every individual gets an opportunity to share their journey, as they reveal joys and pains and how God worked in and through those situations to draw them to himself. After an individual has shared his or her journey, the others surround the person, stretching or laying their hands on them, while they pray or share words of affirmation through Scripture.

A practical tool for this process is for everyone to trace the hand of God in their journey using four categories: Heroes, Heritage, High

---

[4] John White, "What's Better than SASHET?" LK10, May 3, 2015, https://lk10.com/2015/05/03/whats-better-than-sashet/.

[5] Felicity Dale, "A way to deeper fellowship–SASHET," The Blog of Felicity Dale (blog), September 19, 2013, https://simplychurch.com/2013/09/19/a-way-to-deeper-fellowship-sashe/.

Times, and Hard Times. Participants should reflect on a specific phase of their life, such as a decade or a five-year period. Participants can write their responses on a worksheet divided into columns with the following titles:

- **Heroes:** people who have played significant roles.
- **Heritage:** aspects of life where I had no choice, e.g., citizenship, language, culture, early education, or religious upbringing.
- **High times:** things or events that brought joy or accolades.
- **Hard times:** sad events or perceived failures.

After an unhurried time of personal reflection and prayer, each individual creatively shares their journey. Sharing our life story with a supportive body of Christ's followers not only becomes therapeutic and fosters intimacy within a group, but it also helps to provide clarity on God's specific calling.[6]

I personally saw how this exercise broke down many barriers that had existed within a South Indian pastors' fellowship group, which met quarterly over two years. The first few meetings consisted of pastors inadvertently trying to debate and promote their own doctrinal positions, denominational alliances, or areas of ministry. Some of the pastors were planning on withdrawing from the program because they felt the gathering was a veiled attack on their views. However, over the course of two years, as each pastor shared their life story in detail, the differences became secondary. The exercise proved therapeutic, as every pastor received words of acceptance, encouragement, and prayer. The bond that developed among them grew well beyond the two years, and many continue to keep in touch with one another.

---

[6]   Paul Pettit, ed., *Foundations of Spiritual Formation* (Grand Rapids, MI: Kregel, 2008), 217–44.

Share Through Communion

The early Jerusalem church, comprising three thousand people who gathered after Pentecost Sunday, was made up of people from the Jewish tradition who were accustomed to celebrating the Passover in their homes for generations. Before Christ, the Passover feast was a family celebration to not only recall God's deliverance of the past (namely the Exodus journey) but also to serve as a reminder of the future fulfilment of the Messiah's first coming. It was in the context of this celebratory Passover meal that Christ instructed the Twelve to remember him as often as they gathered. Therefore, when the disciples began to practice the breaking of bread, rather than the annual feast to which they were accustomed, it was a daily celebration filled with praise and thanksgiving.

> They broke bread in their homes and ate together with glad and sincere hearts, praising God and enjoying the favor of all the people. And the Lord added to their number daily those who were being saved.
>
> ACTS 2:46–47

A golden rule of all interpretation is to view any action in its historical setting, and texts must be interpreted in light of their context. Going by the historical account of the Passover and the practice of the early church, we can surmise that communion was a long, celebratory meal. Nowadays, it has been reduced to a chip, sip, and a thought—a contemplative ritual that is over in a matter of minutes.

William Barclay comments about how different the Lord's Supper has become today:

> It is not in doubt that the Lord's Supper began as a family meal or a meal of friends in a private house…. It was like the Jewish Passover which is a family festival and at which the father and the head of the household is the celebrant. There can be no two things more different than the celebration of the Lord's Supper in a Christian

home in the first century and in a cathedral in the twentieth century. The things are so different that it is almost possible to say that they bear no relationship to each other whatsoever. The liturgical splendor of the twentieth century was in the first century not only unthought of; it was totally impossible.[7]

To recover the essence of sharing together in remembering Jesus' sacrifice and looking ahead to his return, the following are some important aspects of how the New Testament church celebrated communion.

- It was celebrated in homes in the context of a "love feast" with a few families or a household.[8] Children were active participants.
- Clergy or ordained elders did not officiate communion; in fact, neither did the Old Testament "ordained" Priests or Levites during Passover. While fathers presided over the formal responsibility at the table for a short while, women and the family as a whole worked together to prepare for the meal, during which the story of the exodus was recounted informally, which would have had a profound impact on the children.
- Communion wasn't a quiet meditative exercise as we can observe in many church traditions. It was an informal celebratory meal where everyone, including women and children, could converse freely. Think of a Christmas or Thanksgiving family dinner, but with a focus on Christ.

---

[7]   William Barclay, *The Lord's Supper* (London: SCM Press Ltd, 1967), 111–12.

[8]   "A love feast or agape feast was a fellowship meal eaten by Christians in the early church. There is biblical evidence for the practice of these communal meals, during which Christians gathered not just for the sake of sustenance and socializing, but for the sake of fellowship (Acts 2:46–47; 1 Corinthians 11:17–34)." See "What is a love feast?" Got Questions, accessed May 1, 2025, https://www.gotquestions.org/love-feast.html.

- People did not merely reflect on the past event of Christ's sacrificial death on the cross. Communion also served as a reminder of the future hope, in anticipation of the coming king.

Bearing these facts in mind, communion within the context of a whole meal can be extremely edifying. When celebrated as a love feast, it naturally fosters fellowship. Many of us who come from certain Christian traditions may find this suggestion quite unnerving and revolutionary.[9]

Be Wary of Motives

We need to be aware of our motives when we share or serve the Lord. Our motives might not be totally wrong, but they may weaken or taint God's ideal of what community truly means. Below is a list of motives we should be aware of before sharing with others. Although the first two are often unavoidable, we must be cautious of the last four motives, which can be problematic or sinful.

- **Obligation:** This is a form of transactional giving, for example, payment for a service or a commodity. It could also be repaying someone out of a sense of gratitude or duty, because of what one individual has received from another.
- **Need/concern:** For example, consider an individual who works tirelessly through the week with autistic children. Although a weekend opportunity to feed the hungry might present itself, they shouldn't feel obligated to participate just because others, perhaps those in less emotionally demanding professions, are

---

[9] It is beyond the scope of this book to elaborate in more detail on this topic, but president of New Testament Reformation Fellowship, Stephen Atkerson, has written an excellent paper and accompanying video, which compile the thoughts of many scholars and offer helpful further information. See Stephen Atkerson, "Early-Church Lord's Supper: A Weekly Fellowship Meal," NTRF, accessed May 19, 2025, https://ntrf.org/the-lords-supper-a-fellowship-meal/; Early Church Practice Today, "Early-Church Communion: An Actual Meal," YouTube, May 27, 2021, https://www.youtube.com/watch?v=9NBLHk_a9LY.

doing so. While it may be good that an immediate concern prompts us to meet a need, consistently prioritizing every need we encounter is unsustainable, as the needs around us are endless. (See the section below "Be Wary of Dependency" for suggestions on how to respond to the needs around us.)

- **Compulsion:** Giving may be prompted by an emotional appeal by a preacher or a good fundraiser. Or we may feel compelled to join a choir or music team because the majority of those around us seem more inclined to that gifting, rather than focusing on using a talent God has given us.
- **Guilt:** We may give to a charitable cause or mission to soothe our guilt for living a self-centered life.
- **Control/manipulation:** Sometimes we give because we have been subtly manipulated by others. For example, during the Dark Ages, people were coerced to give, believing it would buy their way to heaven. In contemporary culture, the false teachings of the "prosperity gospel" suggest that God will bless us with financial prosperity when we give to him sacrificially.
- **Acclaim/approval:** Using our gifts of music or even praying in public can be done with the intent of gaining the applause and admiration of others.

Giving motivated by anything other than the grace of God will not please the Lord. In Matthew 6, Jesus shows that even righteous acts can be tainted by hypocrisy, pride, and self-righteousness, revealing that God examines our attitudes and motives, not just our actions.

Be Wary of Dependency

In giving and sharing, we must remember that our primary objective is to ensure people are empowered to function on their own and not be perpetually dependent on benefactors. The popular comedian Trevor Noah gives an interesting twist on the oft-repeated saying, "Give a man a fish, and he'll eat for a day. Teach a man to fish, and he'll eat for a lifetime." He adds: "What they don't say is, 'And it would be nice if you gave him a fishing rod.' That's the part of the analogy that's missing."[10]

Providing handouts to alleviate immediate needs is a temporary, quick fix. In the long run, it creates a culture of dependency that perpetuates the cycle of poverty. It is more valuable to address the root causes of poverty and empower individuals or communities to become self-sufficient. Therefore, genuine sharing may sometimes require refraining from offering hasty handouts that only address immediate needs. Instead, it is better to first listen and observe to understand the root causes of the problem. Subsequently, as God leads, we can provide tools and opportunities to learn. A more lasting impact involves intentionally taking the time to share ideas, resource materials, or connecting individuals with resource persons to teach skills. Over time, the needy can learn to support themselves and function more effectively, and in turn, equip others. However, this approach demands sacrificial service, as demonstrated by Saroj and Bandanna. It would have been far easier for them to offer periodic aid or to have raised funds for the impoverished people of Mong Pong village. But, if they had done this, they would not have had the same lasting impact. The sacrificial service and the gospel embodied in Saroj and Bandanna's lifestyle continues to bring about long-term transformation in Mong Pong and beyond.

When sharing stems from God's grace, it is not motivated by external pressures. We share from an overflow, undeterred by potential losses. Trouble, hardship, or financial challenges will not stop a person activated by the overflowing, superabundant grace of God. God's grace enables us to share our lives and resources joyfully, without restraint.

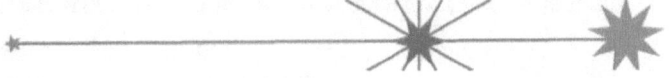

---

[10] Trevor Noah, *Born A Crime: Stories from a South African Childhood* (United Kingdom: John Murray Press, 2016), 180.

Try It Out

Below are a few practices to begin incorporating sharing in your TEAMS.

- **Try sharing life stories/SASHET:** Given the busyness of everyday life, it may be ideal to designate a weekend with the team to devote yourselves to sharing your life stories in an unhurried manner and pray for one another. Periodically incorporate SASHET to foster genuine fellowship centered on Christ.
- **Examine your motives in financial giving or the use of your gifts:** If you become aware that you are not giving from the overflow of God's grace, you may need to change the way you give or the practical outworking of your gifts and talents.
- **Celebrate communion, New Testament style:** In preparation for this meal, consider asking everyone to study how Jesus celebrated the last supper in Luke 22:7–38. If unsure about how to share in communion, you may want to read and gather more information about this practice. Once you feel ready, plan a celebratory meal. Before the meal, have one of the members share the reason everyone is gathered, and make a special reference to the bread and wine, which are symbolic of the risen Christ. After giving thanks for the bread and wine and the food, which should be laid out, people can begin sharing the food, including the bread and wine. As everyone eats, the host could invite people to share about their journey with Christ or a significant truth they've learned about him recently. Take note, celebrating communion this way will be difficult if the table is too long or accommodates too many people. Ideally, there should be a maximum of twelve people, but a smaller number is better to facilitate conversations. This may initially feel awkward for some, especially if they have been used to a different format for taking communion. However, it can be an effective way to begin appreciating the way the New Testament church community celebrated communion.

Meditate and Discuss

Reflect on what the following verses reveal about sharing.

- "Do not be hardhearted or tightfisted toward them. Rather, be openhanded and freely lend them whatever they need.... Give generously to them and do so without a grudging heart; then because of this the LORD your God will bless you in all your work and in everything you put your hand to" (Deut. 15:7–8,10).
- "Honor the LORD with your wealth, with the firstfruits of all your crops; then your barns will be filled to overflowing, and your vats will brim over with new wine" (Prov. 3:9–10).
- "But when you give to the needy, do not let your left hand know what your right hand is doing, so that your giving may be in secret. Then your Father, who sees what is done in secret, will reward you" (Matt. 6:3–4).
- "Command those who are rich in this present world not to be arrogant nor to put their hope in wealth, which is so uncertain, but to put their hope in God, who richly provides us with everything for our enjoyment. Command them to do good, to be rich in good deeds, and to be generous and willing to share" (1 Tim. 6:17–18).
- "And let us consider how we may spur one another on toward love and good deeds, not giving up meeting together, as some are in the habit of doing, but encouraging one another—and all the more as you see the Day approaching" (Heb. 10:24–25).
- "Above all, love each other deeply, because love covers over a multitude of sins. Offer hospitality to one another without grumbling. Each of you should use whatever gift you have received to serve others, as faithful stewards of God's grace in its various forms" (1 Pet. 4:8–10).
- "Therefore encourage one another and build each other up, just as in fact you are doing" (1 Thess. 5:11).

 *Any Questions?*

 *Any Ideas?*

Anything That Touches Your Heart?

CONCLUSION
Spark TEAMS, Make Disciples, and Be the Church Wherever Life Happens

Knowing all the facts about discipleship will not suffice; we will only see real transformation when these principles are applied with God's help. This concluding chapter will summarize some of the discipleship themes in this book and highlight some practical steps to help you live as God's agent of change. We need to remember:

- God has graciously appointed us to follow his example, and serve along with him, to carry out his mandate of making disciples, in an environment of love and acceptance (Matt. 28:19–20).
- We must strive to be with Christ as perpetual learners, or disciples, trusting God to refine us as we go out to serve in his strength (Mark 3:14–15).
- Ultimately, only the Lord knows those who are his (2 Tim. 2:19). Jesus himself advised the disciples against the idea of trying to prematurely uproot the weeds from the wheat (Matt. 13:24–30). Our primary foci should therefore be on cultivating our own authentic faith, discipling others, and fostering unity within the church.

Time to DIE

As we study Scripture, specifically the Gospels, we need to note how God demonstrated his love through Christ and how Christ focused on the few. It is far better to align with what is described in Scripture than to rely on what has evolved in our church strategies and methods over time. Following Jesus' example is a lifelong journey. It takes time, effort, and willingness to put others before ourselves. We can become more like him and make a positive difference in the world around us as we seek to prayerfully apply the practical steps suggested throughout this book in order to multiply Christlike teams. Prayer is an essential part of following Jesus' example. We need to continually maintain an attitude of prayer, seeking guidance and wisdom to draw, influence, and empower people to shine for him.

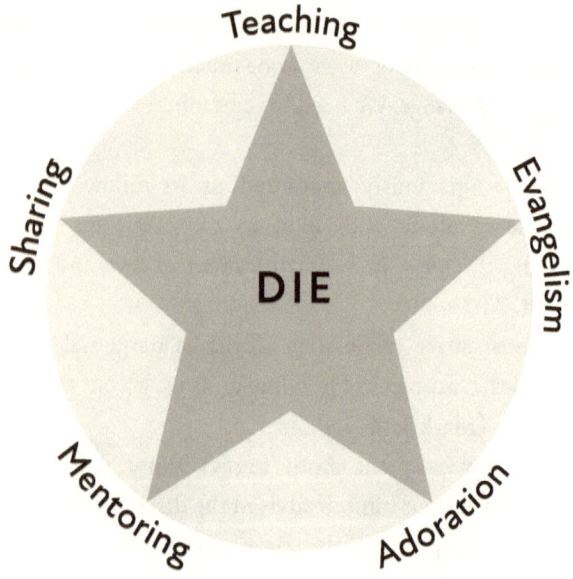

Draw

To *draw* others to Christ, start with the following:

Build friendship, observe, and listen. One of the most effective ways to draw others to Christ is to build authentic friendships with them. Listen to their stories, show genuine interest in their lives, and be a supportive presence on their journey. Value and cherish the friendships you have formed, even if they do not lead to immediate decisions. We need to avoid sharing factual knowledge in a hasty manner. Building genuine relationships will significantly open doors of communication.

Enjoy common activities. Find activities or hobbies that you and your friends enjoy doing together. Whether it's exercising, cooking, playing sports, or board games, spending time together in fun and meaningful ways can help strengthen your relationships.

Serve with unconditional love. Follow Jesus' example by serving others with unconditional love, regardless of their choices concerning Christ. Look for opportunities to help those in need, whether through volunteering, offering a kind word, or simply being present for someone experiencing difficulties. Your love and service may plant a seed that will grow over time.

Pray for the miraculous. Pray for God to do miraculous things in your life and the lives of those around you. Pray authoritatively against the forces of darkness. Pray that God would transform hearts and bring healing and restoration.

Share what God is doing. Be bold in sharing how God has answered prayer at various junctures of your life, while gauging your listeners' interest. Depending on their response, you can proceed to share more about God's offer of salvation.

Influence

To *influence* others for Christ, start with the following:

Prayerfully select a few. Pray for discernment as you identify those who are open to hearing about Christ. Invest your time and energy in those who show genuine interest and willingness to learn.

Enjoy hospitality. While a follower of Christ can take great pains to create a welcoming environment, it can inadvertently put people on edge, particularly those of other faiths. Instead, enter their environment and see God at work in their lives, while receiving their hospitality (e.g., Jesus visiting Zacchaeus in Luke 19:1–10, and Peter in Cornelius' home in Acts 10).

Schedule meetings. Set aside regular times to connect with God and with one another when you gather (ideally in homes, but any suitable location can work), to encourage one another in your faith journeys. Your time together could include Bible study, prayer, worship, and sharing personal testimonies. Celebrate victories while spurring one another on. Take time to follow up and create a culture of mutual accountability.

Commit to TEAMS (see part two on TEAMS). Establish clear goals and expectations for your group and work together as a team to achieve them. Be intentional about supporting and encouraging one another along the way.

Empower

To empower others to serve Christ, start with the following:

Delegate responsibilities gradually. As your group grows, delegate responsibilities to others to help share the workload. This can include planning events, coordinating prayer or worship times, or facilitating discussions.

Evaluate and provide feedback. Regularly evaluate your progress as a group and provide constructive feedback to help each other grow and improve.

Encourage and strengthen one another. Pray for each other and offer support and guidance when needed.

Launch other teams. As your group grows and matures, consider sending out pairs of people to start new groups in other areas (Luke 10).

Celebrate progress. Celebrate progress and achievements as a community by periodically gathering all the teams from a region together for a time of worship, prayer, and sharing.

These principles can be applied in various contexts, whether you are building relationships with friends, family, colleagues, or even strangers. It starts with each one of us *drawing* people toward Christ and then appointing a core team who are interested. We can then focus our attention on this team to further *influence* them with God's love by our example. We can gradually *empower* the team to serve others, enabling them to do the same, and ultimately initiating a chain reaction that makes a lasting impact in the world.

Commit to TEAMS

Our efforts as a team start with the foundational truth that the church is not merely an audience of spectators but rather an active community of Christ's disciples. The early Jewish believers dispersed all over the Roman Empire, even before the apostles did (Acts 2:7–12; 8:1–3). They proclaimed the gospel wherever they went, even without an organizational structure in place. Spontaneous expansion occurred because people continued their commitment to God by devoting themselves to the TEAMS functions we have explored in part two of this book. The apostles, including Paul and many others, subsequently served as catalysts to launch and strengthen local teams of disciples across the Roman Empire.

These functions can be practiced within families, as couples, or even individually. The following are some practical action steps to help strengthen our commitment to Christ. Now that we have gained a glimpse of how God demonstrated his love through Christ, we can begin taking steps to follow his example.

Start as an individual. Practicing these functions—teaching, evangelism, adoration, mentoring, and sharing—individually will make the gathering even more fruitful. The success of any team is directly proportional to every member's personal commitment to spiritual disciplines and how they complement and work together. Likewise, when Christ's disciples come together, the quality of the gathering and outreach is largely dependent on how every member devotes themselves to the functions that have been described. The team becomes a support group of fellow learners, enabling them to mutually edify and spur one another to stay on course.

Gradually build a team. Start with those closest to you who are enthusiastic about following Christ or who display some interest. Don't hesitate to begin, even if only one other person gets involved. Keep in mind that the team should remain small, ideally no more than fifteen members.

Create additional teams. While the team is being formed, encourage everyone to form additional teams within their own spheres of influence. There is no prescribed formula or set number of sessions. Instead, allow for an organic growth of teams, as people respond to God through his Spirit.

Focus energy on the team. It is critical to prioritize time and energy to sustain these groups, because large events can easily override this simpler and more effective approach. The lure of instant gratification from large crowds can steer us away from our commitment to an unassuming team, which has the potential to bring about lasting fruit.

Teaching

We need a commitment to *obey* the Scriptures, as described in Matthew 28:20, rather than merely listening, reading, discussing, or engaging in Bible studies. Reading and studying are good, since faith comes by hearing (Rom. 10:17); but a life of wisdom demands taking God at his Word and obeying it. This means teaching should focus not only on imparting knowledge but also on instilling a desire to follow God's Word and apply it in everyday life. Fostering a culture of obedience within a group setting helps believers grow in wisdom and understanding and allows them to be transformed by the power of God's Word.

Evangelism

A vibrant relationship with the Triune God will prompt Christ's disciples to testify about what God accomplishes in and through them. As people show interest, we can share bite-sized truths about Jesus to arouse their curiosity to read the Gospels with us or a few others. They can discover Christ for themselves. This approach is more appealing than attempting to share the gospel like a marketing campaign.

Adoration

Praise and prayer can be ingrained in every facet of our personal lives and must be incorporated when the team gathers. Music to accompany praise songs can be helpful, but that need not be the only way we praise God. We can use several other creative ways, such as thanking God in a sentence or two, or writing our own psalm. Sketching, painting, and sharing experiences of God's faithfulness are some of the additional ways to give worth to God.

Praying for various spiritual and physical needs within families, the community, and beyond can be a regular feature of team gatherings. Practicing silence and solitude within the group setting to discern the voice of God can also be meaningful.

Mentoring

Mentoring will take place naturally when a team meets consistently, intending to grow closer to the Lord and fulfill his mission. However, just as Christ focused his energies on Peter, James, and John, it can be even more meaningful to meet in a smaller group, beyond the regular team gatherings. As trust develops within this smaller setting, members may feel more comfortable being vulnerable. This openness provides the mentor with deeper insights into individual needs, enabling them to tailor their motivational approaches more effectively and foster stronger connections that support growth. Mentors need to be secure in their identity and relationship with God, since much of their ministry takes place behind the scenes, not on a stage. A mentor's task is to help others shine, as they point them to Christ.

Sharing

A lifestyle of sacrificial service and sharing cannot be forced, programmed, or manipulated. Sacrificial service arises from a life surrendered to God's abundant grace. A close-knit community that meets one another's needs cannot go unnoticed; it has the potential to positively impact society.

Sharing is not limited to monetary contributions. Hasty humanitarian efforts without prayer are not a wise approach either. The root causes of scarcity must be analyzed, and appropriate action must be taken in accordance with God's clear direction and consideration of team members' specific calling and gifting.

Children, Marriages, Funerals, and Other Practical Issues

One of the first questions most Christians ask when discussing the potential of smaller groups functioning as the church are matters related to "hatching, matching and dispatching"—a humorous way to summarize children's ministry, marriages, and funerals. Questions related to leadership structures and handling finances also arise. These issues arise in any pioneering church-planting efforts, including traditional brick-and-mortar church plants, and must be clarified as membership grows. We must remember that *love* precedes leadership. As Lee Wood, founder of 1Body Church[1] and mentor of key leaders in launching small house churches to spread the gospel, often says, "It's always relational before organizational." All these issues can be worked out in prayer, taking the local context into consideration. Below are some brief suggestions to deal with some of these practical issues.

Create an affiliation. Affiliating with an existing legacy church or an organization that understands and validates this approach may be a helpful option, which implies that we affirm the other entity's ministry. Functioning as a home church or focusing on church as

---

1   "1Body Church," 1Body Church, July 16, 2024, https://www.1body.church.

teams, as suggested throughout this book, does not require us to dismiss any other form of church.

Set up a network. If a region has multiple teams, a network of interdependent teams could be formed. They could jointly work out the details as to how various practical issues can be addressed. For example, representatives from various home churches might work together to initiate a kids' club or youth ministry.

Rethink how you disciple children. Parents need to instill the value of *being the church*, rather than *getting ready for church*. This requires intentionality in discipling their children and imparting biblical truths as they face various situations (Deut. 6:6–7). This involves investing adequate time with the family. The practice of family altar—a regular time for Bible reading, prayer, and worship within the home—as a frequent feature of family life, can also inculcate biblical truths. When meeting with other church families, children can participate in times of worship and sharing. An intergenerational community of Christ-followers can naturally provide opportunities for children to learn to interact and have meaningful conversations with people of every age group. They can gain inspiration from the example of older youth and adults, rather than conforming to peer pressure.[2]

Dealing With Erroneous Teachings and Practices

Encouraging or empowering teams may seem foolish, given the threat of various false doctrines and ideologies. It may seem like well-established legacy churches—with a leadership team of theologically trained pastors and clear "statements of faith" displayed on their church websites—are immune from such threats. However, before addressing the issue in relation to small teams functioning as churches, we need to remember that many denominations and legacy churches,

---

[2]   "House church Basics Pt. 7: What About Children?" SimpleChurch Journal, accessed February 3, 2025, https://www.simplechurchjournal.com/2004/03/house_church_ba_3. html.

along with their leaders, have fallen away, despite all their protective measures and organizational structures. The recent scandals involving famous church leaders have not only affected their own organizations, churches, or denominations, but have also made headlines in mainstream media across the world. No church form is exempt from the Devil's attacks. Wherever there are people, sin and Satan are present. Jesus, Paul, Peter, and other writers repeatedly warned about deception infecting the church:

> Jesus answered: "Watch out that no one deceives you. For many will come in my name, claiming, 'I am the Messiah,' and will deceive many."
>
> MATTHEW 24:4–5

> The Spirit clearly says that in later times some will abandon the faith and follow deceiving spirits and things taught by demons. Such teachings come through hypocritical liars, whose consciences have been seared as with a hot iron.
>
> 1 TIMOTHY 4:1–2

> But there were also false prophets among the people, just as there will be false teachers among you. They will secretly introduce destructive heresies, even denying the sovereign Lord who bought them—bringing swift destruction on themselves. Many will follow their depraved conduct and will bring the way of truth into disrepute. In their greed these teachers will exploit you with fabricated stories. Their condemnation has long been hanging over them, and their destruction has not been sleeping.
>
> 2 PETER 2:1–3

So, although erroneous teaching may well infect TEAMS, the fallout or damage may not be as intense as it is with legacy churches, denominations, or organizations that are hierarchically structured. When a church has programmed its members to be passive consumers for years or even centuries, the chances of the whole denomination or legacy church veering off course are much higher, especially when the leadership goes astray. Ori Brafman and Rod Beckstrom, in their book *The Starfish and the Spider*, point out how hierarchical agencies (represented by the spider) can die when their head is decapitated. However, a decentralized network (represented by the starfish) can regenerate itself when an arm is severed.[3] Therefore, while the risk of erroneous teachings and practices exists within networks of teams that function as churches, their decentralized nature offers a significant advantage in limiting their spread.

Given the fact that all forms of church are susceptible to erroneous teachings and practices (as emphasized by Christ and the apostles), we would do well to pay attention to how the Gospels and the Epistles not only edified and warned the church but also provided practical insight on how they were to protect themselves. For example, they established local leadership through the appointment of deacons (Acts 6:1–7) and elders (Acts 14:23; Titus 1:5–9; 1 Tim. 3:1–13; Phil. 1:1). Additionally, the repeated visits and periodical letters (the numerous Epistles such as Romans, Corinthians, Galatians, Ephesians, etc.) strengthened the churches by addressing specific issues and providing ongoing guidance.

The functions of TEAMS, outlined in part two of this book, will help protect against the onslaught of the evil one. For example, the *teaching* function encourages each individual to be grounded in and obey God's Word, equipping them against deception (1 John 4:1–3). As another example, the *mentoring* function—emphasizing healthy interdependence rather than an exclusive "holy club"—can help us discern theological misalignment both within ourselves and among our team members. Or consider how the *adoration* function fixes our gaze upon the majesty and holiness of God, recalibrating our hearts and minds to his perfect truth. These practical steps, mirroring the wisdom of the early church, can prevent teams from going astray.

---

3   Ori Brafman and Rod A. Beckstrom, *The Starfish and the Spider: The Unstoppable Power of Leaderless Organizations* (New York, NY: Penguin Books, 2006).

Ultimately, our commitment is to have a posture of continuous learning and a willingness to yield to God's leading through his Word, his Spirit, and his people.

Make Disciples and Be the Church Wherever Life Happens

With a deeper understanding of discipleship and our collective function as the church, I am hopeful that these principles will spur us on to persistent action, regardless of outcomes. Just as the Thessalonian Jews recognized the transformative impact of Paul and his team, declaring, "These men who have turned the world upside down have come here" (Acts 17:6 ESV), may we also do the same by following Christ's example. We need to place our unwavering trust in God, the ultimate source of all growth and genuine transformation. Only he can bring true change. In his power, may we spark TEAMS, make disciples, and be the church wherever life happens. Let us turn the world upside down, serving confidently as his ambassadors. Let his kingdom come, let his will be done, on earth as it is in heaven.

AFTERWORD
Varughese John

Growing up as a missionary kid in the rural and semi-urban landscapes of South India, I learned early that cultures do not respond equally to the gospel. Each context—with its histories, complexities, and hopes—receives the message of Christ differently. But one pattern remained unmistakable: Those at the periphery of power, those overlooked or oppressed, consistently found the gospel to be redemptive and life-giving. In the margins, the message of Christ has always found fertile ground.

South Asia today is in the throes of rapid urbanization. Cities swell, cultures collide, values shift, and identities are renegotiated. With these shifts come unique challenges—and incredible opportunities—for discipleship and mentoring. These changing realities require the gospel witness to be flexible and contextually relevant rather than functioning from rigid and set ways. Danny Sathyadass's work is a testament to this as it considers the church's witness to be a movement rather than a monument.

In addition to the challenges posed by rapid urbanization, the rise of religious fundamentalism—both in South Asia and globally—adds a layer of complexity. For religious minorities, this often translates into legal and social restrictions, curtailing their freedom to practice their faith. In India, despite the Constitution's guarantee of the right to profess, practice, and propagate one's religion, several states have enacted so-called *Freedom of Religion* laws that effectively limit these freedoms. As a result, pastors and believers in many regions face imprisonment simply for practicing or sharing their faith. Reports indicate a troubling increase in unjust arrests and growing hostility toward Christians. Nevertheless, the call for Christians remains unchanged: to bear faithful witness, even in the face of opposition.

The task before us is not merely to preserve the gospel message but to *live and transmit it* in ways that make sense to the people around us. Christ-followers are called to be ready—in season and out of season. In Acts 17, Paul was not in Athens to preach but was just waiting for Timothy and Silas to arrive. Yet, his response in Athens provides a striking model of contextual *evangelism on the move*. Paul discerns and responds to the spiritual hunger around him. There he stands—not in the familiarity of synagogues but in the sophisticated heart of Greek intellectualism. Athens reminds us that the call to ministry doesn't always wait for the perfect setup. Like Paul, we are called to meet people where they are, to engage cultures thoughtfully, and to speak gospel truth with boldness and grace—or as Danny says, to make disciples and be the church "wherever life happens."

In 2 Timothy 4, we find Paul nearing the end of his journey. Writing his final letter from prison, possibly around the age of sixty, Paul's tone is sober yet resolute. He does not expect to die of old age but faces the real possibility of execution. "For I am already being poured out like a drink offering, and the time for my departure is near," he writes (2 Tim. 4:6). This is the voice of a man finishing strong. These final instructions to his spiritual son Timothy carry weight, urgency, and enduring wisdom.

In parts one and two of the book you have just read, Danny explored the foundational principles of God's draw, influence, and empower (DIE) and the practical outworking of teaching, evangelism, adoration, mentoring, and sharing (TEAMS) as essential for vibrant disciple-making. Now, I want to reflect on three foundational themes that shaped Paul's charge to Timothy—*calling, character, and competency.* These are not only crucial for faithful leadership in an ever-changing world. They also serve as the threads that empower us to live out the DIE principles, effectively engage the TEAMS functions, and embark on a meaningful journey of discipleship and mentoring.

Calling: a divine commission (2 Timothy 4:1-2). "In the presence of God and of Christ Jesus ... I give you this charge: Preach the word; be prepared in season and out of season."

Paul roots Timothy's ministry in nothing less than the authority of God and the return of Christ. This is not a job assignment or a casual encouragement—it's a solemn, divine commissioning. Our calling to serve and lead in the body of Christ is a high and holy calling. It originates not from human systems, institutions, or denominational expectations but from the very heart of God.

If we forget the divine nature of our calling, we begin to misplace our loyalties. We start building kingdoms of our own, mistaking Christian ministry for a career path rather than a sacred vocation. In cultures with a strong honor-shame dynamic, like many in South Asia, this can manifest as an overemphasis on what people and institutions think, rather than what God thinks. Christian work becomes a stage for recognition, comfort, or security. Our leadership becomes marked by hidden fears, unmet emotional needs, and the temptation to impress rather than serve.

Let it not be so with us!

As Danny explores in the first part of this book, to truly embrace our divine calling demands a fundamental "death to self," not as a one-time event but a continuous surrender of our own ambitions, desires, and comfort to the supreme authority of God.

To all who serve—whether pastors, teachers, mentors, or leaders—I offer Paul's same charge: Take up your spiritual leadership with the weight and seriousness it deserves. Preach the Word. Be

faithful, whether it is convenient or not. Do not let your circumstances define your obedience. The call of God is never circum-
stantial—it is always rooted in the eternal purposes of Christ.

Character: the anchor of integrity (2 Timothy 4:3–5). "But you,
keep your head in all situations, endure hardship, do the work of an
evangelist, discharge all the duties of your ministry" (v.5).

In both of his letters to Timothy, Paul places great emphasis on
the personal life of the leader. In 1 Timothy 4:16, he exhorts Timothy
to "watch your life and doctrine closely." Leadership in the church is
never just about what we teach—it is about how we live. As Danny
has consistently noted throughout the book, our life is a visible illustration of the gospel. Our choices, attitudes, and integrity serve as a
living curriculum for those we disciple.

Character is not optional—it is essential. Without it, even the
most gifted leaders become hollow. While the world today celebrates
charisma, the church of Christ is called to cultivate character—the
kind that remains steadfast amid cultural confusion and personal
hardship. This call is particularly relevant in contexts where individuals
may be prone to deifying and following charismatic "performers"
rather than upholding the quiet strength of true character, especially
in a land where gurus often command large followings, as is the case
in India.

Paul knew that ministry was hard. He had been beaten,
shipwrecked, mocked, and betrayed. And so he tells Timothy: *Keep
your head high. Endure hardship. Fulfill your calling.* This is a call to
emotional maturity, resilience, and quiet courage. It's a call to live
before the audience of One and to see a smile on his face. As Danny
says in chapter one, "the life of a disciple is not always marked by miraculous walks on water. More often, it resembles the Twelve straining
at the oars on a stormy sea. It is in this steadfast commitment—even
amid the struggle, even where there seems to be no answer—that
we demonstrate our willingness to follow Jesus. Sometimes our

willingness to follow will involve stepping out of the boat; other times, it will require persisting in rowing."

Character also involves being ruthlessly honest. So we ask ourselves: *What sin remains unconfessed? What pain needs healing? What mask are we still wearing?* As we respond to the Spirit's suggestions, we leave no sin unaddressed but bring it under the purview of the Holy Spirit's searchlight. The high calling of God leaves us with no option but to yield to the Spirit of God—the resident Counselor and the Spirit of Truth—to heal and restore us. Leadership that is not rooted in holiness will eventually collapse under the weight of its own contradictions.

Competency: the stewardship of skills and faithfulness (2 Timothy 4:5-8). "Do the work of an evangelist, fulfill your ministry.... I have fought the good fight, I have finished the race, I have kept the faith" (v.5,7 ESV).

In his final words, Paul doesn't speak of his accomplishments, followers, or legacy projects. He speaks of faithfulness. He fought the good fight. He finished the race. He kept the faith. Competency in ministry is not just about skill—it is about finishing strong. It involves the faithful stewardship of the gifts and responsibilities entrusted to us. We are called to *fulfill* our ministry, not merely to start well. This includes practical skills, such as teaching the Word, engaging in evangelism, fostering adoration of God, offering mentoring, and facilitating the sharing of resources. But it also encompasses deeper spiritual strengths, including the ability to persevere, adapt, grow, and serve with joy.

We often forget that our competencies come from God. Some are given five talents, others two, and still others one. The number doesn't matter—faithfulness does. We do not define our calling by our natural ability. Rather, we define our competency by our *dependence* on the God who equips us. One of the most powerful lines in Acts 4 is this: "They recognized that they had been with Jesus" (v.13). As Danny notes, Christ's followers were identified by their "connection to Jesus, not outward displays." Competency begins not in a classroom but at the feet of Christ. It always remains rooted in our connection to the true Vine. In 1 Corinthians 1:27, Paul reminds us that *God chose the foolish to shame the wise, and the weak to shame the strong.* So, let our goals be God-sized, not me-sized. Let our dependence on God increase as our responsibilities grow.

Christianity in South Asia or anywhere else does not suffer from a lack of workers. It suffers from a distracted workforce—leaders who have traded calling for comfort, character for compromise, and competency for convenience. We face a crisis not of opportunity but of focus. Many have forgotten that ministry is not about personal gain but about kingdom faithfulness.

This "afterword" is not a farewell but a *charge.* As we look to the future of discipleship and mentoring, we must return to these three foundations:

- **Clarify our *calling*:** Know who has called us and why. We must keep returning to that divine commission.
- **Guard our *character*:** Be ruthless with sin, sincere in repentance, and consistent in holiness.
- **Build and sharpen our *competency*:** Hone the skills God has given us. Do not settle for mediocrity—press on to excellence for his glory.

As Paul said to Timothy, I say to you: *Preach the Word. Endure hardship. Fulfill your ministry. Fight the good fight.* Keep the faith. Finish the race. And may the day come when, like Paul, we too will hear these words from our Master: "Well done, good and faithful servant. Enter into the joy of your lord" (Matt. 25:23 NKJV).

AFTERWORD
Alan Hirsch

What you've just read is not simply a book about disciple-making—it's a field manual for the recalibration of the church as we've come to know it. In *Spark Teams*, Danny Sathyadass has taken us on a journey that is both theological and deeply practical, both biblically faithful and culturally attuned. The fruit of decades of on-the-ground experimentation and costly obedience, this book offers a fresh vision of what it means to be the church in real time and real space—wherever life actually happens.

At the heart of this vision is a reframing of what the church is and how it lives. Through the DIE and TEAMS frameworks, Danny reminds us that disciple-making is not an ancillary program of the church—it is its very essence. He returns us to the New Testament's original assumption: that every follower of Jesus is not just a recipient of grace but a participant in God's mission, empowered to reproduce, serve, and lead in the places they already live, work, and play.

There is a prophetic edge to this book that deserves careful attention. Like the parable of the Xerox machine in the introduction, Danny challenges us to see how the church has often been preoccupied with reproducing outdated forms while ignoring the revolutionary spiritual potential sitting latent within the people of God.

Spark Teams is a plea to remember that God has already given us everything we need to get the job done. The movement potential is already baked into the design of the body of Christ—it just needs to be activated.

And here's what I love most: This book is not abstract theorizing. This is embodied theology. Danny's stories are not sanitized or idealized—they are messy, complex, human, and glorious. Whether it's the church that met in the early hours of the morning after a call-center shift in Bangalore, or the faithful witness of Poojappa, the "man of worship" who broke caste barriers through his quiet fidelity to Jesus, each narrative testifies to the power of the gospel when it is unleashed through ordinary people taking Jesus seriously.

Danny also honors the historical legacy of disciple-making movements. His engagement with early Methodism is not nostalgic but catalytic. He rightly sees in Wesley's bands and classes a blueprint for the church as movement—structured yet relational, communal yet scalable. And he is unafraid to name the systemic forces, whether ecclesial or cultural, that so often sap the life out of movements by replacing empowerment with control, and mission with maintenance.

This book is also very timely. In a moment when the institutional church in many parts of the world is facing a credibility crisis and an identity vacuum, *Spark Teams* points us upstream—to the roots of the Jesus movement and the DNA that animated it. It offers a post-clerical, Spirit-infused imagination of church that is fit for purpose in a fluid, decentralized, and post-Christendom age. It is especially encouraging to see how Danny frames this not as a Western export but as an indigenous expression of faith arising from and responsive to the complex pluralisms of South Asia and the diaspora beyond.

Let me say it plainly: If we are serious about seeing the church become a disciple-making, people-mobilizing, city-transforming force again, we need to read this book carefully. And then we need to act on it. So here's the invitation: Start where you are. Gather a few others. Devote yourselves to the Word, to prayer, to one another. Lean into the rhythms of draw, influence, and empower. Practice the communal functions of teaching, evangelism, adoration, mentoring, and sharing. Be the church. Not in a building. Not on a Sunday. But wherever life happens.

Because the church was never meant to be a monument. It was always meant to be a movement.

ACKNOWLEDGMENTS

Writing a book was never something I envisioned early in life. But then again, I shouldn't be surprised—my life verse has always been Ephesians 3:20: "[God] is able to do immeasurably more than all we ask or imagine, according to his power that is at work within us." To him who enabled me, I give all the credit and glory.

This journey began in 2005, when we planted Radiance—the church at Whitefield, Bangalore. From the very beginning, my wife, Sayanora, and our three sons, Joash, Joel, and John, were my closest of "teams." Though the seeds of this book were planted back then, the deep, lived understanding of what it means to sacrificially serve together has grown through the years—and continues even now. We are far from perfect. As a husband and father, I know I fall short in many ways. But I remain deeply grateful to Sayo and our family, who graciously forgive me, cheer me on, and stand with me. My heartfelt thanks to Olivia, my daughter-in-law, and now to Hannah, for their gentle words of encouragement.

I remain ever grateful to Neill Mims, who first sparked my thinking about movements, and to The Dales for their ongoing encouragement and practical help. A big thank you to Dave Coles and to Sayo for the initial rounds of editing and proofreading. The consistent prayer support of Nick Foley and Alwin Robey was immensely helpful, especially during trying times. Thankyou!

Thanks to Rich Robinson of the Movement Leaders Collective and later to Emma Cotterill, who nudged me toward 100 Movements Publishing. I am deeply indebted to the 100 Movements Publishing team—especially Anna Robinson, whose suggestions and editorial insights sharpened the book and made it more focused and appealing. Thank you also to Brenna Varner for her valuable guidance.

This project would not have been possible without the prayers and contributions of many individuals and groups. Special thanks to the late Dr. Wendell Calder, A3, Radiance, Psalm 133, the Hebron staff, Theologians Without Borders, Citylight, extended family, and parents.

I'm immensely grateful to all who endorsed this book, and I offer a special word of thanks to Joe Handley Jr., Alan Hirsch, and Varughese John for their insightful and encouraging words in the foreword and afterwords—they will be a blessing to all who read them.

APPENDIX

Beyond a Building
Tracing the Impermanence of Sacred Spaces
in the Biblical Narrative

God has always communicated with his people, regardless of physical structures. This appendix traces how God has continually interacted with humanity throughout the biblical narrative, highlighting his consistent presence and desire for relationship, even though the channels and contexts for that communication have changed over time.

The Pre-Tabernacle Era

From Adam until the tabernacle was built, the Lord used various ways to communicate with his people. They, in turn, relayed the information to the next generation.

- **Supernatural Means:** God used dreams, visions, and other supernatural ways to communicate with his people. For example, God spoke to Abraham in a vision (Gen. 15:1), and Jacob encountered God in a dream (Gen. 28:10–17).
- **Altars:** The patriarchs built altars at various locations to commemorate God's supernatural intervention, which also

served as a reminder for several generations. Noah built an altar after the flood (Gen. 8:20), and Abraham built altars in Shechem (Gen. 12:7), Bethel (Gen. 12:8), and Hebron (Gen. 13:18).

- **Word of Mouth:** Each generation passed on the story of their lineage and their commitment to Yahweh to the next generation. Godly men like Noah, Abraham, Isaac, and Jacob passed on their insights; and their descendants in turn passed on the story of their heritage to their children. For instance, the people of God were aware of their identity even after being enslaved in Egypt for over four hundred years. God told Moses to introduce himself by saying: "The LORD, the God of your fathers—the God of Abraham, Isaac and Jacob—appeared to me" (Exod. 3:16).

The Tabernacle and Temple Era

The tabernacle was built at God's command during the Exodus journey. It was not just a symbolic representation; it was also a place from which he communicated with his people. God periodically used this structure to commune with Moses and the people of Israel, though he did not limit himself to this venue alone.

God's response to David's desire to build a temple was more of an allowance of David's request than a requirement. Even before consenting, God said:

> I have not dwelt in a house from the day I brought the Israelites up out of Egypt to this day. I have been moving from place to place with a tent as my dwelling. Wherever I have moved with all the Israelites, did I ever say to any of their rulers whom I commanded to shepherd my people Israel, "Why have you not built me a house of cedar?"
>
> 2 SAMUEL 7:6–7

God instead promised that David's throne would last forever. "Your house and your kingdom will endure forever before me; your throne will be established forever" (2 Sam. 7:16). Solomon eventually built the temple. The following are some notable observations:

- It was a national government-funded project with international assistance.
- It was built during the time of peace and prosperity.
- It existed for less than one thousand years.
- The prophets and Christ himself periodically called for repentance and cleansing because of the sin and false religiosity its leaders propagated.
- It was destroyed multiple times during wars. The Romans destroyed it in 70 AD. Subsequently, Muslims took control of the Temple Mount, and today two mosques stand there.[1]

These details illustrate parallels with contemporary situations and highlight the inherent impermanence of such structures, even today. For example, during British colonial rule in India, numerous cathedrals were constructed with international funding and governmental approvals. Similarly, following India's independence, many influential Indian church leaders and organizations secured substantial Western financial support and obtained necessary government approvals to construct church buildings. Although these facilities continue to be a visible testament of the Indian church's positive influence on culture, education, and medicine, it's not hard to foresee that these may not continue. The rising hostility toward Christians in India today has made foreign contributions and government approvals difficult, if not impossible. This mirrors a broader trend, as evidenced by increasing persecution and destruction of church buildings in various parts of the world. For example, in August of 2024, over four thousand Rwandan church buildings were closed.[2]

---

[1] "The Jewish Temples: The First Temple – Solomon's Temple," Jewish Virtual Library, accessed March 23, 2025, https://www.jewishvirtuallibrary.org/the-first-temple-solomon-s-temple.

[2] Wycliffe Muia, "Rwanda shuts 4,000 churches in safety crackdown," BBC, August 2, 2024, https://www.bbc.co.uk/news/articles/c6p2p9dkdzxo.

The Synagogue Era

During the Exile and the silent years before Christ came into the world, the Jewish diaspora constructed synagogues wherever they went, providing local centers for households to learn about their heritage and the Law. Twelve men were required to build and maintain a synagogue, which implies that there was most likely a minimum of twelve households in each area.

Both Jesus and Paul extensively used synagogues as platforms to proclaim the gospel of the kingdom, but these venues were only briefly available before synagogue rulers expelled and sometimes violently persecuted the followers of Christ. Jewish believers, influenced by the Law and the temple structure, eventually became divisive to the early church, as addressed in the books of Galatians and Hebrews.

While the temple and the tabernacle served as large, central gathering places, synagogues offered localized spaces for smaller Jewish communities dispersed throughout the region. This could be likened to our modern local church buildings, which serve regional communities. Like spiritual lighthouses, they help to sustain spiritual fervor. However, with the advent of megachurches, many local churches lose their members. Along with other issues, aging church members struggle to manage local properties due to financial constraints. Consequently, many local churches are merging with "successful" megachurches or selling their facilities to commercial entities.[3] Some of these former places of worship are now temples, mosques, or pubs.

The Homes Era

Christ did not limit his ministry to designated holy spaces like the temple or the synagogue. He intentionally sent out his disciples to identify households in various towns and villages, and their homes

---

[3] Levi Secord, "Wal-Mart Churches and the Need for Community," Front Porch Republic, September 4, 2019, https://www.frontporchrepublic.com/2019/09/wal-mart-churches-and-the-need-for-community/.

served as temporary mission bases (Luke 9–10). After the disciples shared the gospel of the kingdom with their hosts, the host's household then continued to be a beacon of hope for the community. Even as early as Luke 9, Herod heard about the apostles' powerful witness and the miracles accompanying their ministry across the region.

> So, they set out and went from village to village, proclaiming the good news and healing people everywhere. Now Herod the tetrarch heard about all that was going on. And he was perplexed.
>
> LUKE 9:6–7

Early Christian communities frequently gathered in private homes, demonstrating the church's initial reliance on personal hospitality rather than dedicated buildings.[4] Whenever the apostle Paul spoke of the church, he referred to a regional area where believers customarily met in different homes.

A moderately affluent first-century home could hold about thirty people quite comfortably.[5] While estimates vary, scholars acknowledge that one home could accommodate no more than eighty people, with all the rooms in use. In 1 Corinthians 14:23, Paul mentions that the "whole church" came together, implying that the believers met in smaller groups at other times. As Robert Banks writes:

> In any event we must not think of these various types of community groups as particularly large.... Even the meetings of the "whole

---

[4] Examples include the upper room in Jerusalem, the home of John Mark's mother, which served as an early meeting place (Acts 12:12), and the house of Lydia in Philippi, where Paul and his companions were welcomed (Acts 16:15). Similarly, Titius Justus in Corinth, whose home was next to the synagogue, opened his doors to believers (Acts 18:7); and Aquila and Priscilla, wherever they traveled, maintained a church in their home (Rom. 16:3–5). See Michael Green, *Evangelism in The Early Church* (Grand Rapids, MI: Eerdmans, 1970), 208.

[5] Robert Banks, *Paul's Idea of Community: Spirit and Culture in Early House Churches* (Peabody, MA: Hendrickson Publishers, Inc, 1994), 35.

church" were small enough for a relatively close relationship to develop between the members.[6]

The apostles valued gathering together in any available space, including upper rooms, temple courts, homes, synagogues, by the river, the hall of Tyrannus, and even in the house where Paul was arrested. Despite the value of gathering, there is no record of the apostles or any early believers initiating building projects to house the growing number of believers. However, there are emphatic statements that were contrary to the prevailing practices of the day. For example, Stephen's last few words before he died were:

> However, the Most High does not live in houses made by human hands. As the prophet says:
>
> "Heaven is my throne,
> and the earth is my footstool.
> What kind of house will you build for me?
> says the Lord.
> Or where will my resting place be?
> Has not my hand made all these things?"
>
> ACTS 7:48–50

Paul affirms that as believers we are God's building and the temple:

> For we are co-workers in God's service; you are God's field, God's building.
>
> 1 CORINTHIANS 3:9

> Consequently, you are no longer foreigners and strangers, but fellow citizens with God's people and also members of his household, built on the foundation of the apostles and prophets, with Christ Jesus himself as the chief cornerstone. In him the whole building

---

6   Banks, *Paul's Idea of Community*, 36.

is joined together and rises to become a holy temple in the Lord. And in him you too are being built together to become a dwelling in which God lives by his Spirit.

EPHESIANS 2:19–22

Don't you know that you yourselves are God's temple and that God's Spirit dwells in your midst? If anyone destroys God's temple, God will destroy that person; for God's temple is sacred, and you together are that temple.

1 CORINTHIANS 3:16–17

Peter and John proclaim God's people as a kingdom of priests:

You also, like living stones, are being built into a spiritual house to be a holy priesthood, offering spiritual sacrifices acceptable to God through Jesus Christ.

1 PETER 2:5

But you are a chosen people, a royal priesthood, a holy nation, God's special possession, that you may declare the praises of him who called you out of darkness into his wonderful light.

1 PETER 2:9

You have made them to be a kingdom and priests to serve our God, and they will reign on the earth.

REVELATION 5:10

These radical statements throughout the New Testament challenge us to foster movements of God's people to *be* the church rather than construct monuments of sacred spaces to *house* the church.

BIBLIOGRAPHY

1Body Church. "1Body Church." July 16, 2024. https://www.1body.church.

A3 Leaders. "We Are A3." Accessed February 2, 2025. https://www.a3leaders. org/.

Atkerson, Stephen. "Early-Church Lord's Supper: A Weekly Fellowship Meal." NTRF. Accessed May 19, 2025. https://ntrf.org/the-lords-supper-a-fellowship-meal/.

Balasubramanian, Roshne. "Breaking Bondage." *The New Indian Express*. June 9, 2021, https://www.newindianexpress.com/cities/chennai/2021/jun/09/breaking-bondage-2313469.html.

BandLab Singapore Pte Ltd. "I Now Give Up." Danny Sathyadass. ReverbNation. November 2010. http://www.reverbnation.com/dannysathyadass/song/2788756-i-now-give-up.

Banks, Robert. *Paul's Idea of Community: Spirit and Culture in Early House Churches*. Peabody, MA: Hendrickson Publishers, Inc, 1994.

Barclay, William. *The Lord's Supper*. London, UK: SCM Press Ltd, 1967.

"BDB Hebrew: 6951. לְהָק (Qahal)—Assembly, Convocation, Congregation." Accessed April 23, 2015. http://biblehub.com/bdb/6951.htm.

Bonhoeffer, Dietrich. *The Cost of Discipleship*. 1989 ed. London, UK: SCM Press Ltd, 1937.

Bosch, David J. *Transforming Mission-Paradigm Shifts in Theology of Mission*. Maryknoll, NY: Orbis Books, 1991.

Brafman, Ori, and Rod A. Beckstrom. *The Starfish and the Spider: The Unstoppable Power of Leaderless Organizations*. New York, NY: Penguin Books, 2006.

Britannica. "Synagogue, Definition, History, and Facts," Britannica. Accessed March 8, 2025. https://www.britannica.com/topic/synagogue.

Cambridge Dictionary. S.v. "confidence." Accessed April 9, 2025. https://dictionary.cambridge.org/dictionary/english/confidence.

Cambridge Dictionary. S.v. "freedom." Accessed April 9, 2025. https://dictionary. cambridge.org/dictionary/english/freedom.

Cambridge Dictionary. S.v. "legal." Accessed April 9, 2025. https://dictionary. cambridge.org/dictionary/english/legal.

Challies, Tim. "Faith Hacking: The Swedish Method." Challies.com. September 1, 2014. https://www.challies.com/christian-living/faith-hacking-the-swedish-method/.

Chambers, Oswald. "Usefulness or Relationship?" My Utmost For His Highest. Accessed September 15, 2022. https://utmost.org/usefulness-or-relationship/.

Coleman, Robert E. *The Master Plan of Evangelism*. Old Tappan, NJ: Revell, 1963.

Coleman, Robert E., Bobby Harrington, and Josh Patrick. *Revisiting the Master Plan of Evangelism*. USA: Exponential Resources, 2014. https:// my.exponential.org/ebooks/revisitingmasterplan/.

Collins Dictionary. S.v. "empower." Accessed May 18, 2022. https://www. collinsdictionary.com/dictionary/english/empower.

The Cooper Institute. "Legendary 'Father of Aerobics' Dr. Kenneth H. Cooper Turned 90." Cooper Institute. May 12, 2021. https://www. cooperinstitute.org/2021/05/12/legendary-father-of-aerobics-dr-kenneth-h-cooper-turned-90.

Crossman, Ashley. "McDonaldization and Why Sociologists Are Not Lovin' It." ThoughtCo. June 27, 2024. https://www.thoughtco.com/mcdonaldization-of-society-3026751.

Dale, Felicity. "A way to deeper fellowship–SASHET." The Blog of Felicity Dale. September 19, 2013. https://simplychurch.com/2013/09/19/a-way-to-deeper-fellowship-sashe/.

Dimond, Sydney G. *The Psychology of the Methodist Revival*. 6th ed. London, UK: Oxford University Press, 1926.

"Discovery Bible Study: A Safe place to see for yourself what the Bible says." Accessed February 12, 2024. https://www.dbsguide.org/.

Early Church Practice Today. "Early-Church Communion: An Actual Meal." YouTube. May 27, 2021. https://www.youtube.com/watch?v= 9NBLHk_a9LY.

Encyclopedia.com. S.v. "essenes." Accessed March 11, 2025. https://www. encyclopedia.com/philosophy-and-religion/judaism/judaism/essenes.

Faithward. "Lectio Divina: An Ancient Contemplative Spiritual Practice." Accessed May 9, 2025. https://www.faithward.org/lectio-divina-an-ancient-contemplative-spiritual-practice/.

Foster, Richard J. *Celebration of Discipline.* Revised 1988. New York, NY: HarperCollins Publishers, 1978.

GIGM, "The Incomparable Christ." Growing in Grace Ministries. March 15, 2009. https://gigm.org/news/the-incomparable-christ/.

Global Slavery Index. "India, Global Slavery Index." Accessed May 13, 2022. https://www.globalslaveryindex.org/2018/findings/country-studies/india/#footnote:12.

Got Questions. "Why, When, and For How Long Was the Apostle Paul in Arabia?" Accessed April 25, 2025. https://www.gotquestions.org/Paul-in-Arabia.html.

Got Questions. "What is the right hand of fellowship (Galatians 2:9)?" Accessed May 14, 2025. https://www.gotquestions.org/right-hand-of-fellowship.html.

Got Questions. "What is a love feast?" Accessed May 1, 2025. https://www.gotquestions.org/love-feast.html.

Green, Joel B., Scot McKnight, and I. Howard Marshall, eds. *Dictionary of Jesus and the Gospels: A Compendium of Contemporary Biblical Scholarship.* Leicester, UK: InterVarsity Press, 1992.

Green, Michael. *Evangelism in The Early Church.* Grand Rapids, MI: Eerdmans, 1970.

Halloran, Kevin. "Jim Elliot's Journal Entry with 'He Is No Fool...' Quote." Anchored in Christ. October 28, 2013, https://www.kevinhalloran.net/jim-elliot-quote-he-is-no-fool/.

Hirsch, Alan. *Disciplism: Reimagining Evangelism through the Lens of Discipleship.* Cody, WY: 100 Movements Publishing, 2004.

Hirsch, Alan. *The Forgotten Ways: Reactivating Apostolic Movements.* Grand Rapids, MI: Brazos Press, 2016.

Jacobson, Richard. "What Constitutes a Real Church?" YouTube. October 17, 2013. https://www.youtube.com/watch?v=ZGmeIUK4xpE.

Jackson, Thomas, ed. *The Works of John Wesley.* London, UK: John Mason, 1829.

"John 6 Vincent's Word Studies." BibleHub. Accessed August 23, 2022. https://biblehub.com/commentaries/vws/john/6.htm.

Jewish Virtual Library. "The Jewish Temples: The First Temple – Solomon's Temple." Accessed March 23, 2025. https://www.jewishvirtuallibrary.org/the-first-temple-solomon-s-temple.

Karthikeyan, M. "Adaiyaalam Documentary, Pain of Bonded Labour, Iyan Karthikeyan, Irular Tribe." YouTube. February 9, 2021. https://www.youtube.com/watch?v=gugkerCPO5U&t=10s&ab_channel=KarthikeyanM.

King, Alison. "From Sage on the Stage to Guide on the Side." College Teaching, Vol 41(1), 1993.

Koessler, John. *True Discipleship: The Art of Following Jesus*. Chicago, IL: Moody Publishers, 2003.

Küng, Hans. *The Church*. Garden City, NY: Image Books, 1976.

"Leadership and Influence, Icma.Org." Accessed August 25, 2022. https://icma. org/articles/pm-magazine/leadership-and-influence.

Limbu, Bijaya. "Traditional Village Marriage System of the Nepal, Limbu Culture, Bijaya Limbu." YouTube. March 5, 2022. https://www.youtube. com/watch?v=aDphCVHCDdU.

LK10. "10:2b Prayer." Accessed November 29, 2022. https://lk10.com/ tag/102b-prayer/.

Mabilog, Patrick. "Here's a simple Bible-Reading format you can follow." Christian Today. April 28, 2016. https://www.christiantoday.com/article/ heres-a-simple-bible-reading-format-you-can-follow/84936.htm.

Metcalf, Sam. *Beyond the Local Church: How Apostolic Movements Can Change the World*. Downers Grove, IL: InterVarsity Press, 2015.

Meyersohn, Nathaniel. "How Xerox Became a Verb." February 2, 2018. https:// money.cnn.com/2018/01/31/news/companies/xerox/index.html.

Mui, Wycliffe. "Rwanda shuts 4,000 churches in safety crackdown." BBC. August 2, 2024. https://www.bbc.co.uk/news/articles/c6p2p9dkdzxo.

Navertise. "The Lord's Supper: An Actual Meal and Lamb's Marriage Supper Type." Small Churches, BIG Impact (NTRF). August 3, 2016. https://ntrf. org/the-lords-supper-a-fellowship-meal/.

Navigators. "How to Study The Bible." Accessed May 13, 2025. https://www. navigators.org/resource/how-to-study-the-bible/.

Navigators. "Prayer Walk." May 14, 2025. https://www.navigators.org/resource/ prayer-walk/.

Noah, Trevor. *Born A Crime: Stories from a South African Childhood*. United Kingdom: John Murray Press, 2016.

Pebam, Ringo. "How Steve Jobs Got the Ideas of GUI from XEROX." YouTube. January 4, 2014. https://www.youtube.com/watch?v=J33pVRdxWbw.

Pettit, Paul, ed. *Foundations of Spiritual Formation*. Grand Rapids, MI: Kregel, 2008.

Phillip, George. Personal Interview. February 2014.

Saroj, Rai. Zion School. Personal Interview. February 16, 2023.

Sathyadass, Danny. "I Now Give Up." Produced by BandLab Singapore Pte

Ltd, ReverbNation. November 2010. httpps://www.reverbnation.com/dannysathyadass/song/2788756-i-now-give-up.

Secord, Levi. "Wal-Mart Churches and the Need for Community." Front Porch Republic. September 4, 2019. https://www.frontporchrepublic.com/2019/09/wal-mart-churches-and-the-need-for-community/.

Shultz, Timothy. *Disciple Making Among Hindus: Making Authentic Discipleships Grow*. Pasedena, CA: William Carey Library, 2016. www.missionbooks.org.

SimpleChurch Journal. "House Church Basics Pt. 7: What About Children?" Accessed February 3, 2025. https://www.simplechurchjournal.com/2004/03/house_church_ba_3.html.

Snyder, Howard. *The Radical Wesley and Patterns of Church Renewal*. Downers Grove; IL: InterVarsity Press, 1980.

"SOAP – Easy Bible Study Method (Individual or Small Group)." My Salvos Toolkit. Accessed February 12, 2024. https://my.salvos.org.au/toolkit/resource/easy-bible-study-method---soap--individual-or-small-group-method/624/.

"Strong's Greek: 1743. Ἐνδυναμόω (Endunamoó)—to Empower." Accessed May 18, 2022. https://biblehub.com/greek/1743.htm.

"Strong's Greek: 1849. Ἐξουσία (Exousia)—Power to Act, Authority." Accessed May 18, 2022. https://biblehub.com/greek/1849.htm.

Thayer, Joseph, and James Strong. "Thayer's Greek: 1577. Ἐκκλησία (Ekklésia)—Assembly, Convocation, Congregation." Accessed April 23, 2015. http://biblehub.com/thayers/1577.htm.

ThoughtCo. "McDonaldization and Why Sociologists Are Not Lovin' It." Accessed October 4, 2022. https://www.thoughtco.com/mcdonaldization-of-society-3026751.

Thru the Bible with J. Vernon McGee. "Dr. J. Vernon McGee." Accessed October 6, 2022. https://ttb.org/about/dr-j-vernon-mcgee.

Thru the Bible with J. Vernon McGee. "From Home Groups to Churches: The Gospel Travels a New, Old Path." Accessed October 6, 2022. https://www.ttb.org/global-reach/home-groups.

Travel Log. "Limbu/Limboo Documentary from Sikkim India." YouTube. July 28, 2018. https://www.youtube.com/watch?v=v7elPxOJnuI.

"Usefulness or Relationship? My Utmost For His Highest." Accessed September 15, 2022. https://utmost.org/usefulness-or-relationship/.

Vennard, Jane E. "The Breath Prayer." The Upper Room. Accessed May 14, 2025. https://www.upperroom.org/resources/the-breath-prayer.

Viola, Frank, and George Barna. *Pagan Christianity*. USA: Tyndale House Publishers, Inc, 2008.

Warren, Rick. *The Purpose Driven Church: Every Church Is Big in God's Eyes*. Grand Rapids, MI: Zondervan, 1995.

Watson, David. *Discipleship*. London, UK: Hodder and Stoughton, 1981.

Watson, David, and Paul Watson. *Contagious Disciple Making*. Nashville, TN: Thomas Nelson, 2014.

Wesley, John. *Explanatory Notes upon the New Testament*. London: Epworth, 1958.

White, John. "What's Better than SASHET?" LK10. May 3, 2015. https://lk10.com/2015/05/03/whats-better-than-sashet/.

Wigton, Lance. *Laying a Solid Foundation Before Planting a Disciple Making Church*. Real Life Ministries: Church Training and Development.

Wilde, Ronald, and Phillip Messina, "Leadership and Influence." ICMA, May 3, 2019. https://icma.org/articles/pm-magazine/leadership-and-influence.

Wilkins, Michael. *Following the Master: A Biblical Theology of Discipleship*. Grand Rapids, MI: Zondervan, 1992.

Word Resounds Today. "About." Accessed May 13, 2025. https://www.wrtoday.org/about-us.

Word Resounds Today. "The History and Story of TWR, Trans World Radio." Accessed February 26, 2015. http://www.twr.org/about/history.html.

World Vision. "Our History." Accessed February 15, 2024. https://www.wvi.org/our-history.

ZDNET. "PARC Scientist Recalls Jobs' Famous Xerox Visits." YouTube. November 11, 2011. https://www.youtube.com/watch?v=ZOF-j6Nxm04.

DONOR LIST

This would not have been possible without the prayers and contributions of the following people. Thank you again!

A3
Amit Kumar
Christina Moore
Christopher Gnanakan
Daniel Jeyachandran
Emma Cotterill
Ian W. Payne
Jaison Aby Cherian
Jaison Cherian
Joy Christina R
Krishna Durairaj
Radiance
Rich Robinson
Sanjay John Thomas
Santosh Gnanakan
Stancy Abraham
The Dales
Tony Plews

Citylight

citylightglobal.com

Citylight began in 2020 to spark **Christ-centred, decentralized yet interdependent teams**—functioning as churches wherever life happens.

Through **in-person training** and **online assistance**, we equip leaders and small groups to:

- **Grow deeper** in faith
- **Multiply** teams to function as churches
- **Stay connected** in a reproducing network

📖 **Watch Actified**—our Acts Study Series on YouTube.
This resource is perfect for sparking team discussions about living the early-church vision today.
Search for "Actified by Citylight" on YouTube.

🙌 **Serve**
Your skills, time, and prayers can make an eternal difference.
Join us—serving from **wherever you are.**
✉ sparkteams@citylightglobal.com

❤️ **Donate**
Fuel the mission—help leaders grow and churches multiply.
https://www.tms-global.org/partners-and-projects/details/citylight